WHACK

around the head

Purpose Passion and Power
at work right now!

by

SHARON EDEN

Whack Around The Head
First published in 2010 by
Ecademy Press
48 St Vincent Drive, St Albans, Hertfordshire, AL1 5SJ
info@ecademy-press.com www.ecademy-press.com
Printed and Bound by Lightning Source in the UK and USA
Set in Warnock Pro by Charlotte Mouncey
Printed on acid-free paper from managed forests.
This book is printed on demand, so no copies will be remaindered
or pulped.

ISBN 978-1-905823-85-7

For Adam and Cassie

'Be yourself. Everyone else
is already taken.'

Oscar Wilde

Praise

'Whack Around The Head' helps those of us in business to challenge ourselves to be more, to really find what's important in our lives and take a stand for who we want to be. That makes a positive difference not only to ourselves but all of those around us. A big 'thank you' to Sharon for her stories, exercises, passion and, above all, role modelling of awakening our lives.

Charles Brook, Director, The Performance Coach,
www.theperformancecoach.com

If you're feeling restless and asking yourself if there is more to life but wouldn't be caught dead reading self-development books, *read this one!* Sharon knows what will help you find and live the very best in yourself and her book takes you white-water rafting to personal change. Be prepared for an exhilarating journey with a skilled guide.

Ann Lewis, Director, Ann Lewis Coaching,
www.annlewiscoaching.com

This book is like no other book you have read before. It engages your emotions and your intellect as you explore your own life and, more importantly, your future. This book's simply brimming with insight and authenticity, which can only come from profound personal and professional experience. Sharon shares a number of personal anecdotes in order to encourage us to be honest about our own. This is not like reading a book. It is like a personal and intimate conversation with a close and trusted friend who is completely honest with you. As you read it, you can practically hear her voice.

Stan Hornagold, Director, The Marstan Group,
www.marstangroup.com

'Whack Around The Head' shows you how to be more effective at work and enjoy your job, even if it's not the job of your dreams. It's not a theory book full of unproven ideas. Instead, it's an essential instruction manual illustrated with real life stories to guide your way forward. An excellent mix of the inspirational and practical.

Marina Nicol, Managing Director, OH Works Ltd,
www.ohworks.co.uk

Fun, punchy, engaging, down to earth, inyerface. Good blend of commonsense perspective and profound depth about life. The exercises are great, easy to follow, and Sharon's examples and self-disclosure really give it life.

John Leary-Joyce, CEO, Academy of Executive Coaching,
www.aoec.com

An honest, humorous, down-to-earth conversation between a passionate, wise leader and the reader.

Lise Moen, Director, Nordcape Ltd,
www.nordcape.com

For anyone who thinks there has to be more to life or they are living the wrong life, this is your book. It is a no-prisoners-taken wake-up-call to go out there and live the life you've always wanted to. Buy it for yourself or buy it for your friend. It will introduce you to the real you and give you the life you have longed for.

Simon Horton, Director, World Class Performance Ltd,
www.worldclassperformance.com

Sharon Eden embodies authenticity, passion and joy in her life and her work – she totally exemplifies the subject matter of her book, 'Whack Around the Head'. Like her, this book is fast-paced, challenging when necessary, a strong and reliable resource to friends and clients alike. Sharon's voice rings out loud and clear as a reminder to live a fuller, more purposeful, passionate and satisfying life. This is the kind of book to which one can return, finding new inspiration each time."

Christine Miller MA FRSA, Founder & Editor
ReSource Magazine & The ReSource Foundation
www.resourcemagazine.co.uk
www.resourcefoundation.org.uk

Acknowledgements

My warm thanks to Irene Brankin who delivered me from my desire to be a clinical psychologist and witnessed some of my big whacks around the head. To Roberto Assagioli, Diana Whitmore, Piero Ferrucci and Judith Firman who were the first of my formal teachers in the work.

And to all my teachers, from the renowned to everyday heroes and heroines, including my courageous and inspiring clients.

To my 'writing buddy', Phyllis SantaMaria, for long hours and loving support as we journeyed together writing writing writing. To my partner in crime, Lise Moen, who delights in prodding me fiercely-creatively and defies words in her own determination to live out loud.

To Charles Brook, Karen Moxom and Peter Shotton for their bold tenderness, integrity and companionship over time.

To Julia McCutchen as a catalyst for me lighting fires. And to Mindy Gibbins-Klein for her consistent and powerful support to express my expertise writing *my* way... and just doing it! Not to mention her hand on the publishing helm.

To everyone who's ever helped me believe in me and my purpose. From Mrs Levy, my junior school teacher, to my current international buddies including Dorothy Dalton, Dr Jack King, Wendy Mason, Irina Wardas, Dr Steve Broe, Marion Chapsal, Monica Diaz de Peralta, Colin Lewis, Elizabeth Wieland and Leona LaPerriere. And to all those I've not yet met but will.

To my children, Adam and Cassie, for their unswerving backing and belief in me, their encouragement and great humour. I've been truly blessed by their presence.

And, finally, to 'outtamybox ME' without whom this book would never have been possible...

Contents

Power

So, What If Change Is Scary!

THE END

INTRODUCTION – BURNING HOLES

This book has been burning a hole in me for years. It comes from my own white water rafting and paddling-in-the-sea adventure of developing myself, my purpose, passion and power, both at work and in the rest of my life.

An experience of moving from 'living dead' in a monochrome, stilted movie to being energetically alive in a vibrantly coloured, panoramic spectacular.

People sometimes ask me what I think about reincarnation. I reply that, as I don't remember being physically dead, I don't feel qualified to come down on one side or another of the 'does it happen or not' debate. What I *do* know is I've been reincarnated so many times in *this* life it's more than enough to manage without thoughts of previous ones.

Me coming more and more alive is a continual 'watch this space' journey as each re-invention of myself provides a platform for lift off to the next. You'll never get bored growing yourself!

This book also comes from working professionally with thousands of under-performing and dispirited people at work as a psychotherapist, coach and trainer. My heart and soul ached for them and, as I'd discovered for myself, I was determined to find ways to help them come alive without years and years of therapy and/or coaching.

I remember once giving out leaflets for an event in commuter rush hour near London Bridge and Liverpool Street stations. Orwellian '1984' scenes greeted me filled with glassy-eyed, robotic and grey looking figures streaming like a vast army out from or into the stations, depending on the time of day.

That's no way to live... without enthusiasm, without colour, without vitality!

So, this isn't any old self development or professional 'how to' book. It's a scram bam, whack around the head inviting you to use not just your logical and analytical intelligence to read and work with it, but a whole spectrum of intelligences which go way beyond. And if you're thinking you can't do that, you're wrong!

Remember the time you tried to solve a problem or situation logically without success. Then, you heard the lyrics of a particular song or were pumping iron at the gym or decorating a room or saw something unrelated in a magazine or shop window and... BAM! You got the answer.

Some other intelligence brought extra information to your logical mind which made the solution just drop into place. That some other intelligence could include emotional, sensory, intuitive, synthesising, spatial, interpersonal, intrapersonal, artistic, linguistic, creative, kinaesthetic and who knows what else intelligence.

Famous scientists, artists and inventors throughout history, like Leonardo da Vinci and Albert Einstein, provide evidence for what I call 'whole brain' processing. They used all the above intelligences... and more. Open to dreams, symbols, sensations, metaphors, and things happening outside of themselves, feeding into their overall thinking, logical and illogical.

In fact, whole brain processing goes way beyond what we normally conceive of as our 'mind'. Neuroscience has shown that intelligence is not only located in the brain located in your head but also in cells throughout your body.

Makes sense. If your genetic coding, DNA, exists in every cell of your body, why not your intelligence?

Just think. You're a walking, talking, whole brain, lean and mean processing machine! Even though your education probably only paid attention to your mental, logical, verbal and mathematical intelligences, the rest are there, just a hair's breadth away, waiting for you to develop them.

What possibilities!

For whole brain processing helps you access information and knowledge beyond that you normally connect with using logical intelligence alone. Not only that. It helps you access that information and knowledge more quickly through things like symbols, pictures and metaphors. So, throughout this book, all exercises are designed to stimulate and develop your whole brain processing. Enjoy the adventure and...

To get the most out of the exercises, do them!

If you don't actually do them, read through them. They're so powerful that, to a lesser extent, just reading them will stimulate information and knowledge you might not otherwise have been able to access.

Expect to be surprised and even gob-smacked by what you discover in the process.

Also, please, please make this book your own. Mark it, highlight words, phrases or whole sections, fold down pages and write in margins and white spaces. Interact with its words and messages until you and 'it' end up in the rich conversation you deserve. Because...

Lastly, this book is about YOU!

It's been burning a hole in me for years because I want it to burn a hole in you. Not a 'nice' thing to say? I don't do nice. I do real.

And, I think it's the most passionate, energising, flame filling, life giving hullabaloo gift I can offer... It's here in these pages, from me to you.

YOU, living out loud, the most you can be in only the way you uniquely *can* be. Alive, living your purpose, your passion *and* your power, weaving them together vibrantly to create enjoyment at work not as just a thing you 'have to' do, but a thing you were born to do.

See you there!

CHAPTER 1 – GET READY, GET STEADY...

*'The supreme triumph is to be most vividly,
most perfectly alive.'*

D H Lawrence

The martial arts are a very good place to start for a whack around the head. Physical skills are essential but useless without the ability to be awake. To be vividly alive, able to intuitively predict your opponent's next move and respond positively and swiftly to anything which comes your way.

So, any quality 'sensei' or teacher will tutor his students in the art of 'mindfulness'. This is self-regulation of your attention so you can focus on your immediate experience which then heightens your ability to recognise and respond to events *right now*.

Then and only then can you be totally aware of your current thoughts, feelings and surroundings. This then leads to being able to control your concentration and focus on what you're doing and what's happening right now.

At the same time you're in a receptive state, curious and open to what might happen, able to think laterally, multi-dimensionally and even beyond the... look out, here it comes... 'blue sky' or 'helicopter' thinking.

All of which sound like excellent abilities to have at work too!

The ancient sensei was crafty in his teaching of 'mindfulness'. Students had to practise it by kneeling hour after hour on hard cobbled courtyards concentrating on their current experience, moment by moment.

Imagine that. No moving, apart from blinking. No food or water. Breakfast time was often chosen by the sensei as a great opportunity for practise. No showering or ablutions of any sort. Just focus on your experience in this moment, and this moment, and this moment and this...

And the next, and the next, and the... Just the thought of kneeling on hard cobble stones for hours and hours makes my shins ache with the eventually numbing pain.

No reporting back to the sensei after your allotted hours, "I've done it, sir." To ensure you practised mindfulness, the art of being totally present in the moment, he was constantly there, monitoring you all the time. Moving between the rows of you students, his sharp eyes caught the slightest movement or even a nano-second of glazed over eyes.

Glazed over eyes are worth another mention. They're a common feature of people working in offices, on production lines, physical or intellectual, in boring meetings or doing any repetitive task which requires no more than the skills of a tortoise.

Glazed over eyes mean you're somewhere else. Anywhere but anywhere rather than be in the moment and experiencing the boredom-frustration-disillusionment (replace my words with your own kind of pain) that's going on inside. Or experiencing what's happening in the outside world around you.

When the sensei detected such a glazed over eye or micro-movement, he would leap high into the air with the speed of a marauding tiger, pull a gnarled stick from the cavern of his sleeve and whack you forcefully around the head. Not forcefully enough to cause actual brain damage but forcefully enough.

Such excruciating pain is more than enough to bring you absolutely into 'mindfulness', into experiencing your reality right now!

You crumple with an agonised yelp. And you burn with the lesson that the pain of *not* being present is far more agonising than any pain you might feel from being alert and alive in the moment. It's far more agonising than you being fully awake and experiencing all of what's going on inside and outside of you this minute now.

A technique not to be employed with your work colleagues however desirable it might feel at times!

Now, I can't know exactly what happened in your family. But, after working with thousands of people, my guess is it was a variation, more or less pronounced, of what happened in mine. Nobody in my birth tribe had the faintest idea about being present, experiencing life as it happened or responding creatively to it and each other.

Their behaviour reminds me of the 'sleeping sickness' H G Wells wrote about in one of his books where, after catastrophic inter-galactic war, people wandered blindly, holding onto each other in chains while fast asleep. My family was comatose. They only knew about being 'absent without leave', plodding blindly through the motions of living with the odd highlight here and there. But, mostly, they were disengaged and asleep.

They didn't know that being alert, alive and response-able in the moment like a skilled martial arts' practitioner is veritable heaven by comparison.

Because when you're alert, alive and response-able you're living, *truly* living instead of just existing. You notice colours, textures, sounds, smells, sensations, feelings and even taste vividly rather than living tepidly like an unaware and programmed robot.

Alert and vital, you're also far more aware of what goes on inside your head... and your guts. This means you can have choices in how you think, feel and behave. You can have choices in how you create your life.

Yes... In how *you* create *your* life!

But I didn't learn any of this until my early thirties. And my lesson came through an almighty, humungous you-better-believe-it, Grade A humdinger of a whack around the head.

Unhappily married and with my then husband failing a business spectacularly ... if you're going to do it, do it in style ... we faced the likely re-possession of our home. We had two children to care for and my husband wasn't working. Stir into that disillusionment with the degree I was taking *and* having to work to put food on the table.

Stress, anxiety, fear... outcome unknown! All laced with a great and seductive desire to really stop the world... and get off.

After I crumpled like a martial arts' student with an agonised yelp, I came to my senses in a totally new way. The double whack around my head of the circumstance *and* my suicidal thoughts woke me up big time.

I became skin prickingly alive and realised I'd previously been 'living dead'. I'd been nothing more than an automated zombie blindly going through the motions of living, reacting to people, events and life like an insect speared on a twig.

I'd been controlled by internal 'scripts' constructed from beliefs, attitudes, thoughts and feelings I'd been taught were the right ones to have. I'd been living other people's ideas of what life was about instead of my own. And these ideas had nothing to do with what was actually happening in my reality.

As vulnerable and as shaky as I was at the time, I galvanised myself and my husband into action. I chose to stay in the marriage to see us through. I cleared the house of anything we weren't using for car boot sales... and the recovery began. It culminated in us downsizing, leaving our previous home with a zero balance and a fresh start.

Did I strangle my then husband? Did I stamp my tantrum foot and spit in his food? I so wanted to. Did I want to face getting our family out of a mess? No! I didn't want to do any of that.

What I wanted was a mystery someone else, a magical daydream 'rescuer' to do it for me. Just like you might hope someone or something will magically appear to deliver you from your job.

But that whack around the head woke me up so well that, despite my daydream trances... you'll discover more about them... and my reactions, I remembered the 1970s Billy Ocean song, 'when the going gets tough the tough get going'. And by being aware of events, both inside and outside of me, I made choices. And that's exactly what I did... I got going! I got working on how to get us out of that tough situation.

What about you?

What are the daydream trances you use to avoid taking charge of yourself and your work life? What are the consequences? What's the very painful price you pay for not taking charge?

And when precisely will you get bored of repeating the same old cycles of behaviour again and again?

Make it now!

The down to earth approach of this book is designed to jolt you out of that disempowered 'same old same old' stuff.

Make it now!

Because this book is aching to propel you into getting alert, proactive and supercharged through discovering your purpose, passion and power.

Purpose, passion and power at work?!... Am I crazy?

Yes!

I'm crazy for you to upturn your ideas about how work has to be. I'm crazy for you to put your butt into gear to enthuse your work life and beyond.

Shout the words loudly ferociously quickly...

PURPOSE PASSION POWER!

PURPOSE PASSION POWER!

PURPOSE PASSION POWER!

Notice how your lips, chest and belly pulsate with energy. Notice how the words echo in your head for a second, a reverberating voice with something to tell you. Because it has...

Your purpose is like a lodestar which shows you your way. It's your guiding principle which strongly urges you to act in line with it. It's also like the lodestone which has magnetic properties. It's your earthy magnetic base from which you operate in the world.

So, at the very same time, your purpose both leads you in particular directions and draws you to them as if by magic.

Your passion is your Va-va-va-vrooom! It's your essential life energy, your birthright and heritage. It's what makes the difference between feeling alive or 'living dead'.

And, if you're concerned that passion *has* to be hot and loud, you're mistaken. It can deliciously be so and, equally deliciously, be as soft and light as a feather brushing your cheek.

Your power is about you standing in your own ground, knowing what's right for you, what's not and having the 'will' to take action. But it's not the forceful and pushing, I-don't-care-who-gets-hurt-in-the-process, kind of will you might well have encountered at work.

The 'will' I'm talking about is a flowing certainty like the energy of water turning a miller's wheel. This will is softly strong, adaptively resilient and creative. It takes you through from having a vision and making a choice to create it, to doing so dynamically and with integrity.

The great thing is when your passion and power are aligned with your purpose they don't have to be loud and jarring... unless you want them to be. Your choice! And when the three are lined up, your motivation, engagement and enjoyment with what you're doing, whatever it is, are guaranteed.

This book is not for the lily-livered or faint-hearted. It wields a metaphorical gnarled stick which will indeed whack you around the head from time to time. I can't know how or precisely when. What's a whack for you might not be a whack for someone else.

But, as the martial arts' student discovered, any discomfort you might feel re-connecting with your aliveness, your purpose, passion and power, will be more than worth it. And will be as nothing compared with the pain of just existing.

'Just existing' is that 'down' mood or queasy feeling in the pit of your stomach when you think of work. Or the dread which gets your guts churning. It's irritability or frustration which comes out of nowhere and zaps anyone, however dear to you, within gunshot.

It's numbed out sensations or feeling like a robot or one-step-removed-from-reality-ness. It's thoughts nagging your head off... or low spirits dragging you down... or your lack of motivation... or feeling hopeless or trapped or, even worse, resigned to it all.

You've not picked up this book for no reason!

CHAPTER 2 – STARTING LINE...

'We shall not cease from exploration and the end of all our exploring will be to arrive where we started... and know the place for the first time.'

T S Eliot

Forget any other book you might have read about purpose, passion and power.

Some tell you it'll take forever to find them. Some tell you you're not meant to find them easily as they're only worth having if you have to sweat and struggle to get them.

And some say you have to go on a 'spiritual' journey to find your purpose passion and power. You have to meditate, eat certain foods and pay certain trainers lots of money to instruct you. And then, if you've done everything absolutely right, then and only then, *and* if you're very, very lucky, all will be revealed to you... or not!

I once attended a year's course specifically to find my life's purpose. So I could find its 'true' meaning and what I was supposed to be doing with it. We students strained through exercise after exercise, like a bad case of constipation, trying to discover our unique and magical purpose as defined by the course leader.

Some people got what they thought it was and, whatever they thought it was, it clearly wasn't what they were doing then. Others didn't get it but decided if they moved house, changed their job, changed their partner, bought a new car, had children *then* they'd find purpose and meaning in life. *Then* they'd get rid of the unsettled or frustrated or itchy scratchy sensations they had from time to time.

Others left defeated, disappointed and feeling second class citizens because they never quite got what they believed they were supposed to get as instructed by the trainer. Quite the opposite of being inspired and motivated by finding your purpose, passion and power!

What a waste of time, energy and money because the secret is quite simple....

Very early on in my career I once had a client who couldn't settle. He was a bright and resourceful man in his mid 30s but, whatever job he did, he very quickly lost interest in it. It just wasn't 'him'.

So, he decided to go travelling with the belief that somewhere out there he'd find his purpose and know what he needed to do. Like some of my fellow students on that course, he gave up his job, sold his flat and told his lover he was off and didn't know when he'd be back.

And did he travel! From country to country, from continent to continent, working his way and searching searching searching. Maybe something would show him his purpose. Maybe someone would show him his purpose and what he was supposed to be doing both with 'it' and his life.

This went on for nearly two years until he eventually realised it just wasn't working. He was no nearer finding his purpose than when he first began travelling.

So, tail between legs, he returned home. His family helped him rebuild his life although, not surprisingly, his lover was long gone and his career break needed mending big time.

One day, out of the blue, he called me to make an appointment. He was finally ready to discover his purpose. Because...

He'd been so busy searching outside himself he'd forgotten where his purpose was *really* located... until he stayed still long enough to remember!

And, as you're reading this book, that could be the same for you because...

You don't have to go anywhere where you're not, be anything that you're not or do anything that you're not already doing. You're already absolutely and exactly *where* you need to be, being *how* you need to be and doing exactly *what* you need to do to discover your purpose... and then your passion and your power.

Your purpose is right in front of your nose!

It's just a hair's breadth away!

Where you are in your job right now is absolutely the optimum place. You're exactly at the totally right place to begin to find your purpose.

So start limbering up!

Some questions follow. Please answer them with the first thing which comes to you, however bizarre or nonsensical it might seem.

To explore, you'll be using whole brain processing which includes emotional intelligence, sensory intelligence and intuitive intelligence as well as your usual logical and mental functions.

This means your answers might come in the first instance as words, pictures, colours, sounds or sensations. These could arrive in recognisable or unfamiliar forms.

That's because you'll be using all of your brain including aspects which aren't logical in the way we usually understand 'logical' to be, and they don't necessarily communicate in verbal and logical language.

Remember... the first answers you get are the ones with all the juice!

So, record whatever comes first even if you don't immediately understand it. In the following hours, days or weeks and, especially, as you continue with this book, you will.

1. What do you think about your working life right now?

2. How do you feel about your working life right now?

3. What are you looking for outside of yourself right now?

4. What do you think or imagine that will give you?

5. What's important about that?

6. What will that do for you?

7. If the thing outside yourself was a mirror reflecting back to you something you're not aware of inside yourself... what could that be?

If you've got some very surprising answers, ones you already know, or a mixture... excellent! You're more than ready for the next chapter.

CHAPTER 3 – GET OUTTAYERBOX
HOW DID YOU GET IN THERE IN THE FIRST PLACE?

'When I listen to others' voices and let them control me, I no longer hear my own. I become less of myself.'

e. e. cummings

You're inside a 'box'. You might or might not think that's the case... and it is!

You needed to belong to the family and tribe into which you arrived. You were born with big eyes and large pupils. This was so your 'raisers', parents and/or other people who brought you up, would fall in love with you and make sure you physically survived.

I've seen even the ugliest of babies coo-d over so 'baby eyes' in general are a very effective genetic adaption. Regrettably, however, this doesn't always work due to factors out of the baby's control like having crazy adults being in charge of them.

This just underlines how very vulnerable you are at birth and during childhood. And how important it is for you to have your physiological and safety needs met so you can physically survive.

As you grow your needs to be loved and to belong kick in. And that's when the emotional, mental, psychological and all the other -al and/or –ological needs kick in too.

You learn it's either conforming to the family's or tribe's way of doing things or be rejected. And, unless you want to be, or have the nerve to be, the black sheep of the family, you conform for the sake of survival.

So, you learn to be who, what and how your nearest and dearest teach you to be. You end up believing other people's beliefs, valuing other people's values and living out attitudes, behaviours and other people's lives instead of your own.

Just like a client of mine who was highly artistic and had wanted to go into the arts in some way. His 'business' parents were aghast. 'You'll never make your living that way! Where's the security in those kinds of jobs?' As if there's security in any kind of job these days.

And, as they held the emotional, psychological and financial purse strings, and he needed their approval, he suffered an engineering degree for a quiet life.

Wrong! The quiet life which seems the easy option is the hardest one of all.

Like him, at times you might have felt you'd been born into the wrong family if who and what you are is so at odds with who and what you've been expected to be.

I once listened to the audio recording of a personal development seminar run by an eminent facilitator. He asked the hundreds of people there, "Put up your hand if you feel you were born into your *real* family."

I heard a flurry of movement combined with a deep chuckle from him and distant laughter from the audience. Then I heard him say, "I thought so! Not more than 20% of you think you were born into your real family."

My father split with his family on marrying my mother. And it wasn't until I re-connected with aunts, uncles and cousins in my early 30s that I could go, "Wow... this is my *real* family!"

Most of them were dark haired and more Mediterranean looking like me. Plus they were live wires, often jovial, and when they engaged with you, they *really* engaged with you.

They were so different from the depressed and under-achieving energy of my mother's family. And, although my sister was fair and blue eyed like my mother's side, she believed she was adopted. Because, like me, she suffered through having her 'up' energy turned down by our mother's and grand-mother's disapproval. So how could these people be our real family?

And sometimes you don't notice the difference! Sometimes you happily go along with who and what you're expected to be until something in your life hits you.

Could be a crisis which jolts you... that kind of whack around the head.

Could be having your eyes opened to different ways of living through going to university or travelling. The kind of whack around the head which seems like you've found a whole different universe you never knew existed.

It could be any life event which is sufficient enough to trigger in you the kind of whack around the head that says, "There has to be more to life than this!"

There is!

To discover what that 'more to life' is you need to get outtayerbox. Because everything inside it results from what you were taught to believe is who you are, what you are and what you *should* be doing. It's what you were trained to be and do rather than what you *could* be or do.

And it wasn't just your raisers who influenced how you turned out. There's a whole range of other influences too.

CHAPTER 4 – GET OUTTAYERBOX
IDENTITY'S GREAT WHEN IT'S YOUR OWN!

'Identity theft is one of the fastest-growing crimes in the nation... especially in the suburbs.'

Melissa Bean

So, what is 'identity'?

In this case, identity is your sense of self which provides your experience of the 'sameness' and continuity of your personality over time. It's this aspect which usually gets disturbed in some mental illnesses such as schizophrenia.

And, if you think I gave raisers a bit of a hard time in the last chapter, you'll be delighted to know they're not the only ones who train you to be and do in line with what they think appropriate for you to be and do. There's a whole other range of factors like...

Your raisers' economic and social situation. Clearly, if they had bags of money, you'd have different experiences AND expectations from someone whose raisers had no money to talk of or were midway financially.

And the amount of money your raisers had also influenced what you did for 'fun'. Were you riding horses, even possessing your own, or similar? Or were you playing footie, or similar, at the local public park?

Your raisers' professional status. There's a tendency for people who are doctors, lawyers, and in the military to want their offspring to follow in their own footsteps. That also used to be the case for dockers, miners and watermen... all now greatly reduced professions in the UK.

In some families, you can get a whole dynasty with generations of people entering the same profession as their ancestors whether they wanted to or not.

Your education? Was it prep and private schooling or local state primary and secondary? Your experience and expectations will be influenced not only by your schooling but also the area in which you go to school. And boarding school invites a whack around the head experience all of its own.

And what about the 'poor' kid whose parents bust a gut to get them into private school? If I had a pound for every damaging story I've heard about feeling an outsider, not belonging, shame and ostracisation ... you can imagine the rest. What kind of influence do you think that could have on your identity?

Your friends as you grow up. An ancient therapist once told me that, by the time your children reach 14, you've done all the mothering you can do. Then it's down to their peers. It's down to the friends they've made or, sometimes, more to do with the new friends they make during this period.

My daughter grew up with a bunch of core friends she'd known since she was 6, some of whom are still her closest buddies. In fact, she married one of them. Our families had similar values and similar expectations, like all our children would go to university... which they did.

And beyond that? Some of the group split off finding new friends and different kinds of lives they wanted to live, whether their raisers liked it or not. And, within the group, there's a wider range of differences now due to differing life experiences and other friends they've made.

Then there's the thorny issue of gender. Some research years ago revealed that mothers of all socio-economic classes behave differently from birth with boys than they did with girls. Is this stuff hard-wired?

And, while some enlightened raisers and professionals don't discriminate between the genders with reference to expectations and career influence, it still damn well exists for both genders.

Think about your experience as a male or female. What were you steered towards as a career? What were you steered away from? And, if you were a 'gentle' male or a 'strong' female, answer the question in your own time!

Your choice of career or job also, of course, influences your identity. If you chose to become an IT programmer, a financial analyst, a personnel officer or marketing whizz kid you'll learn behaviours and ways of being necessary for the role. These then get absorbed into your identity, into who you think you are.

Not quite finished with the raisers yet. Because there are other roles you can learn to adopt from the family and tribes, both into which you were born and those you later get to know, which also affect your identity.

There's the 'Career Casualty', always having 'wrong' done to them and always in trouble of one kind or another which 'just isn't my fault.' Or are you a Survivor-Coper who learned life was tough and how to cope with it in your own stoical way. Amazing how that struggle continues, isn't it?

Add to that...

The Clever One who always has to be in the 'right' or at the top of the tree as a measure of success, The Challenger who can be great in a team for stimulating new thought but can go overboard by challenging everything that comes their way or The Tyrant who stomps about with a 'don't do what I do, do as I tell you' attitude. The list of possible roles you could have historically learned how to play is never ending.

You'll probably have one major identity, say, The Organiser who can be great at project management, systems and getting things done. Then you'll have a range of sub-identities, say...

The Rebel, who can be a bit of a maverick and buck the system, The Attention Seeker who constantly needs external validation to feel good or The Mover and Shaker who's great at creating political strategies and alliances.

The list of possible roles you could have historically learned how to play is never ending. It's also not unusual, when we use one identity most of the time, that we get fed up with it and want to be its opposite. When people flip into acting seemingly 'out of character', they shock themselves and usually say, "I don't know what got into me!"

The truth? It wasn't a case of what got into them but rather a case of what sub-identity got out of them.

And so on and so on and so on and so on...

Where is all the purpose, passion and power? It's absolutely there for you when you're in line with who you want to be and when you do what you want to do. And I guess it's there for you if your learned identity is exactly as you want it to be. In my experience, that's rarely the case.

But what happens when any aspect of your trained identity doesn't fit? Were you trained to live your life through being in some-one else's shoes instead of your own? Did you take on an occupation because it was 'the right thing to do', because it was someone else's expectations of what you would do rather than what set your heart on fire?

I just love it when rock stars, specialists, popular artists or highly successful people like Richard Branson tell the story of how they were told by a teacher or someone important to them that they'd never come to much. Wouldn't that just motivate you to prove them wrong? Or would you collapse in defeat and accept their judgement?

Be honest with your answer. It'll tell you something about how your identity got formed.

One of the worst things about having an identity with which you feel out of sync is the situation will slowly eat you alive.

Restlessness, distress and feeling unsatisfied but perhaps not knowing about what or how to change it. Thinking there must be more to life than this. And, at its very, very worst, psycho-somatic physical illness or poor mental health including depression and personality disorders.

So far I've been writing about your identity being formed by influences out of your control. There will, of course, be aspects where you've made a choice like the sports you're involved in... or did you? Like the way you dress... or did you? Whose or what influence led you to those choices and how did they or it influence you?

So, I'm suggesting, for the most part, even when you think you've chosen aspects of your identity, other influences will have been at play.

These would be external influences like the gang or profession to which you belong. And, of course, there would be internal influences through sub-identities like The Negative Critic or The Conformist. All will have played their part in decisions you've made, consciously or unconsciously, about your identity.

Doesn't mean that's bad or wrong. When you've discovered your purpose, passion and power you will definitely choose to take some or maybe even lots of what's already in your identity and make it your own. Throwing the baby out with the bath water is definitely not recommended if you want to stay sane.

And you're probably not there yet!

When you are, you cannot *not* be exhilarated by the freedom of being YOU outtayerbox, of choosing your own identity. You cannot *not* be enthused by experiencing yourself as all joined up and fitting in your skin.

And if you're not there yet, where exactly is the YOU outtayerbox?

CHAPTER 5 – GET OUTTAYERBOX
SO THERE YOU ARE!

'Very often a change of self is needed more than a change of scene.'

Arthur Christopher Benson

YOU are in that half-thought which came as quickly as it went. YOU are in that tip of the tongue sensation. YOU desperately attempts to tell you something but you don't quite get it.

YOU are also in those piercing insights which strike in a flash and disappear just as quickly as inyerbox you censors them. And for some, YOU is the feeling that you don't quite fit the company you keep.

YOU is in the voice which sometimes whispers and, at other times, roars inside your head, even in your body sensations, what it wants and desires. AND which you learned to ignore because it wasn't in line with what you were taught to want and desire.

YOU is that voice which knows exactly what is right for you and not right for you, the direction you need to be going in and the routes to ignore.

YOU is the voice of your essential integrity as a human being.

Imagine you're working on a policy, a strategy, implementing a directive, leading your team or undertaking a project for your boss. And something seriously just doesn't look, sound or feel right.

That's a message from YOU. You're unable to put your finger on what's not OK... but you just know there's something 'off'.

Might be you're recognising a fundamental flaw in the policy, strategy or directive. Might be you have no idea what that 'not OK' is. Whatever... somewhere there's a dissonance between what you're doing-thinking-being inyerbox and YOU who's outtayerbox.

So what if you voiced your disquiet? What if you said, "I'm not sure what it is but something's just not right with this?" What if you stood up, made yourself visible and highlighted the thing ringing warning bells inside... or just that you were having them?

WHO ME?!!!

I'm sick to death with the number of clients who tell me their *WHO ME?!!!* stories. They go something like this...

You see a flaw in something or know what's going on just isn't right. You sound out your colleagues. You sound out your team. Their YOU outtatheirboxes also recognised the flaw or that what's going on just isn't right. So, in discussion with them or not, you decide to take it to your boss or bring it up at the next team meeting, knowing that you're not on your own.

The most usual ending to this story is that everybody else stays quiet. They don't back you up and might even deny they had ever agreed with you.

Very understandable. Their YOU initially responded to your YOU but was then smothered by fears. Fear of being seen as a trouble maker. Fear of standing out from the crowd.

Great herd instinct!

You were taught that if you were different from the rest of your tribe you'll get noticed by a predator, killed and eaten. So you conformed, you made yourself just like the rest of the herd and ended up being eaten alive anyway... from the inside out.

But you know what usually happens to people who put their heads above the parapet. You know what happens to those who buck the organisational culture, the organisational sub-culture, the zeitgeist of whoever's your manager.... ya-di-ya-di-ya.

For what usually happens is further measures are put in place for you to conform and not rock the boat.

Unless, of course, you work in an enlightened organisation or with enlightened people who welcome your outtayerbox contributions. Or you learn that politics can indeed be sexy using your outtayerbox YOU.

Then you can discover how to communicate elegantly and easily, influencing in line with the higher good, benefitting you and the collective of which you're a part... including the human race.

The world needs your outtayerbox YOU!

The kind of thinking which created the world's problems is not going to solve them. The world needs people who are willing to say the un-sayable, discuss the un-discussable and challenge challenge challenge what YOU will know is counter-creative and damaging to all living creatures and the world in which we live.

OK... I've stepped off my soap box! AND that comes from *my* passion. My passion that you grow to be the very most you can be.

I'm not daft. I know not everyone is able or would want to take up the sword and fight the big fight. But what's important to me is that you take up the sword for yourself and your life, carving it through making choices about the way you want it to be.

And, by so doing, you'll be adding your energy, however silently, however big or small, to positive creation and influence for yourself and others.

That's the potential of outtayerbox YOU!

To begin with, even if you know what's causing the dissonance between your inyerbox and outtayerbox YOU, you probably brush your discomfort signals away.

They're like an insistent puppy with a wet nose scrabbling up your trouser leg... or worse.

Imagine you're sitting in a meeting round a highly polished table with papers in front of you, pen in hand and poised all ready to go. You're ready to be informed and contribute.

However, as the minutes tick by, you realise this is yet another tedious meeting where nothing much of any use is going to happen. And your 'ready to go' does just that, in spirit if not in body.

This kind of meeting is about ego stroking and positioning rather than the purpose for which it's been called. A meeting which is about people looking as if they're doing something important, where the 'players' and you know who they are... hey, maybe you're one of them... make sure they get seen and heard. Self-promotional politics reigns.

Then, in the middle of the meeting, something just explodes inside and YOU see how meaningless, ludicrous and what a sham the whole thing is.

> A pompous emperor, who cares more about appearances than anything else, hires two tailors to make him the finest suit of clothes there ever was. What the emperor doesn't know is that the two tailors are con-men.

> They show him the finest, most exquisite cloth in the entire universe. They tell him it can't be seen by anyone who is either a) stupid or b) totally unfit for their position.

> The emperor can't see the cloth but pretends he can for fear of appearing a) or b) or, even worse, both of them. His ministers do the same.

Word soon gets out about this magical cloth and magnificent world beating suit of clothes. And the people can't wait to see their emperor in such a fine spectacle.

When the suit is ready the tailors, unsurprisingly, take their money and hightail it out of the empire. At the same time as they depart, the emperor begins his promised and triumphal procession through the capital showing off his wondrous new clothes.

He's met by his subjects with great rejoicing. They give outstanding ooooooh's and ahhhhh's because none of them want to be seen as a), b) or both either.

However, one small child, who's not yet been fully squeezed into her box, calls out in a loud and shocked voice, "Oooh Mummy, the emperor's showing his willy. He's got nothing on!"

At first, her mother tries to gag her as most adults do when a child states the uncomfortable and unpalatable truth. But, it seems her little truthful voice pierces right through the boxes of some nearby adults. And they start calling out, "The child's absolutely right. The emperor is stark bollock naked!"

And such is the way of things, when there's sufficient consensus, the message spreads like wildfire. However, the emperor, impervious to reality and the cat-calls of the crowd, marches on holding his delusional head high, regardless.

Answer these questions very quickly before you read on and take the first answer which comes into your mind.

Who in your organisation is the emperor?
Who are their ministers?
Who's the child?
Who are the adults who try to gag her?
Who are the adults who get outtatheirbboxes and validate what she sees?
And last but not least...
Who are those very enterprising tailors?

Why on earth did I ask you those questions?

Knowing who's who in your organisation is a big advantage. It helps you weave your way through your current job awake, resourceful and creatively using the roles people play to achieve beneficial outcomes for yourself and others.

The questions were also designed to limber up your connection with outtayerbox YOU.

It's this 'you' who sees and understands way beyond your inyerbox thinking. It's this 'you' who connects with your purpose, passion and power *and* makes them absolutely available at work for you right now!

CHAPTER 6 – GET OUTTAYERBOX
DO IT BEFORE THE WHACK

'We need to find the courage to say NO to the things and people that are not serving us if we want to rediscover ourselves and live our lives with authenticity.'

Barbara de Angelis

That meeting you were attending in the last chapter, what do you do with your meaningless-ludicrous-sham insight about it?

Do you pack it away because a) you don't want to appear stupid (shown up as not having got the point of the meeting when you oh so have!) or b) don't want to appear as unfit for your position for not 'playing the game' or, of course, both?

The tendency inyerbox will be to behave far more like the emperor than the outspoken child who recognises the reality of things. The child who lives from her outtayerbox YOU.

This doesn't mean you necessarily need to leave your job, change your career, change your relationship, move house, and become a belly dancer or an Antarctic expedition adventurer.

What it does mean is that you start listening to yourself and the YOU which points out incongruence. It means you pay attention to the sensations in your body which cause discomfort and the things you see, hear and feel which say...

"HEY... THIS IS OUT OF SYNC WITH ME!"

Those 'internals' can help you discover your purpose, meaning and direction, *and* your passion and power. Because they're messages from YOU outtayerbox about living and working more in line with what floats your boat whatever job you're doing, whatever position you're in now.

And don't tell me you don't have any 'internals'... because you do. It only seems you don't because at some point, even before you can remember, you were taught not to take any notice of them. And the more you took no notice of them, the weaker your muscle of connection with them became.

But, just like doing physical exercise, you can strengthen your connecting muscle. And, by so doing, learn how to recognise, manage and act upon those crucial internal signals.

Sceptics usually find it hard to believe it can be that simple. Well, it is! If you don't want to challenge yourself with the simplicity of it, just keep being and doing same old same old.

Stay in denial. 'Oh, those sensations are just indigestion' , 'Must be the curry I had last night' , 'over exercising' or 'lying awkwardly in bed' excuses for your internal sensations are no excuse at all.

And, if you choose not to pay attention to those sensations, there's something very important you need to know...

If the Universe has a lesson to teach you, it comes knocking on your door. If you don't respond to its knocking and don't open your door, it goes away only to return some time later with the same lesson.

When it does, it knocks and knocks very loudly on your door. If once again you decide not to open your door to that lesson, the Universe goes away. And it, being a persistent little bugger, returns some time later with the same lesson.

When it does this time, it kicks and bangs ferociously with a thunderous energy. And if you still don't want to know, pretend everything's alright la-la-laaaaa, it most definitely returns with a vengeance next time.

Because then it arrives with tornados and tsunamis and, despite all your denial, will, without a shadow of a doubt, break your very resistant door down, rip up your floors, fuse all your electrics and burst every water pipe with a force which also overthrows you.

Welcome to one humungous-Godzilla-full throttle-double-duty whack around the head!

And the shape of the gigantic burning wound on your head and the red suppurating wheal it leaves behind?

Could be your beloved partner telling you they are leaving.

Could be you darkly and deeply suffering clinical depression.

Could be you losing your job.

Could be you devastated to lose your reputation over something you thought didn't matter.

Could be you repeatedly and painfully bypassed for promotions for which you think you're ideal.

Could be you blindly entering a personal or professional relationship which stinks.

Could be you thinking the world or life is against you.

Could be you stressed out of your mind on the edge of going crazy.

Remind you of anything?

Experience has taught me at great cost that the most intelligent and adaptive thing to do is to take note of the tiny whacks, including the internals, before, due to your negligence, they become gigantic screeching banshees or horrendous hurricanes in order to get your attention.

Ignore them at your peril because they are sacred clues. They are crucial messages from YOU outtayerbox which demand recognition, yelling...

HERE I AM!

I AM YOUR PURPOSE, PASSION AND POWER.

I AM YOUR BIRTHRIGHT.

I AM YOUR HERITAGE.

COME GET ME!

So, follow the signposts of your discomfort. Record them faithfully in a little notebook which you carry all the time. Act as if you're Hercules Poirot uncovering the plot... context, content, issue, internal signals... and revealing 'et voila!' the fascinating mystery and miracle of outtayerbox YOU.

Because YOU are the very thing which will lead you to your purpose, passion and power *and* give you precisely what is needed to find them at work right now.

> Remember a time, at work or otherwise, when you had a little whack around the head, a time when you thought or felt something wasn't quite right.
>
> Were you unaware of reality like the emperor? If so, how did you do that?
>
> Were you aware of reality but chose to ignore it, like the emperor's ministers? If so, how did you do that?
>
> Did you speak out, like the child, vocally or by taking action in some way?

If so, who were the 'adults' who got outtatheirboxes to validate and support you?

They could have been real people and/or internal resources like the sub-identities in you which believe in justice and fair play or the courage to speak out.

If you didn't speak out or act, who were the 'adults' who you experienced gagging you?

Again, they could be real people and/or internal sub-identities like the The Negative Critic or The Disciplining Teacher.

And, if you didn't speak out or act, who could have been 'adults' who would have validated and supported you?

Again, they could be real people and/or internal 'voices'.

Finally... when did you last act like one of those very enterprising tailors? And what happened when you did?

What have you learned from doing this exercise?

And because of that learning, what will you do differently when your next little whack around the head occurs?

Just as in the martial arts, outtayerbox YOU helps you to see the little whack around the head before it arrives. Or, if you're not 'mindful' enough to see it coming, outtayerbox YOU can help you to work with it rather than rail against it.

Living from outtayerbox YOU helps you co-operate with the lesson the whack around the head brings... purposefully, passionately and powerfully!

CHAPTER 7 – GET OUTTAYERBOX
ARE YOU MAD???

'The only people for me are the mad ones, the ones who are mad to live, mad to talk, mad to be saved, desirous of everything at the same time, the ones who never yawn or say a commonplace thing.'

Jack Kerouac

Isn't it madness itself when people who are just so alive get labelled 'mad'?

I recently sat on a rush hour Tube train going into central London. People had blank staring and glazed over eyes or closed eyes or eyes hidden by newspapers numbing out the cattle herding. Others, with tinny sounding iPods, ears stuffed with plugs against the world, were doing the same in their own way. Again, with those glazed over eyes.

Isn't this ritual of disconnection for work 'mad' too?

It happens all over the place in cars, buses, trains, even while walking or talking. Your mind's somewhere else, lost in going over past events or going over imaginary things in the future which haven't happened yet. Pining, preparing, picking over and pronouncing on the past and/or the future.

A station announcer's distorted message created some non-comprehending looks. Nobody asked anyone else if they'd heard what the announcer had said. They flicked free newspapers or the FT at each other with derision. Head deep in print, to acknowledge each other would be a step too far.

For many this daydreaming, this trance, is considered 'normal'. And yet you're bypassing your life in the very moments that you're having your trance. You're somewhere else.

Surely, that's madness?

Yet, this isn't the only trance you'll use.

There's the 'being in my business role' trance. And then there's the 'meeting' trance, the 'deadline' trance, the 'office politics' trance, the 'project management' trance. And what about the 'don't you step into my territory' and the 'them against us' trance? Or even the 'executive suite' trance?

How can you inspire, influence and motivate anyone, let alone yourself, if you've put yourself to sleep?

Yes, you do need certain kinds of trances, particularly when you want to concentrate, to focus, to get things done. AND you can be outtayerbox YOU at the same time. You can still be alert and alive to yourself and your surroundings, snapping out of your focusing trance in a nano-second if need be.

Yet, many people live their lives continually moving from one trance to another. Here I am in my 'waking up and getting ready for work' trance. Now I'm doing my 'commuter' trance followed by my 'put on the business face' trance while, all the time, I'm yearning for my 'it's the weekend' trance.

They're all delusions, all 'mad', yet accepted as normal. And isn't it 'mad' that you've learned to be in them most of your waking life? What a waste to spend life asleep!

I'm getting fed up thinking how to say this, write this. I feel restless and irritable, bored that you might even want to stay in those trances. And maybe it's *your* restlessness, irritability and boredom with which I'm connecting.

Maybe they're *your* little whacks around the head, coming from your hidden desire to have you and your life be different. Maybe it's that hidden desire which you squash with boredom.

Squashing with boredom is like an anaesthetic. It makes the pain more dull and manageable somehow... although not less painful in the long run.

That pain comes out in many ways.

I've lost count of the number of clients I've worked with who've been like spitting cats around the office and at home. It wouldn't take much to trigger their irritability.

Oh yes, they could put it down to stress, but blaming your behaviour on something and not taking response-ability for it gets you nowhere. It only gives you a seeming excuse, a self justification for your spitting cat behaviour.

And, in reality, there are no excuses for behaviour harmful to others... and yourself. Because that behaviour certainly is!

People differ in the issues which lie behind their spitting cat behaviour. However, very often, boredom with themselves and their lives is a common theme. The 'trances' they act out are killing them and the pain is coming through anyway

Creative challenge is *always* present. So... you're being bored and boring. You're sleeping on the job of your personal evolution as well as your organisation's... and both your futures are at stake.

This is a dynamism alert!

Without it there is no creativity, no innovation, no growth and no inner leadership. No connection with your outtayerbox YOU, the source of your purpose, passion and power and your natural ability to be alive and effective.

Experiment with this...

> Get to know the stages of this exercise really well so you can do them without thinking. And remember, using whole brain processing, take the first answer you get however initially bizarre those answers might seem.

> Choose one of your favourite trances. Could be your 'going to work' trance, your 'in boring meeting' trance, your 'listening but not listening to someone' trance or even your 'I'm angry' trance.

Now, close your eyes and let your body move into the position it has when you're in your favourite trance. Just trust your body. It will automatically shift position to match your trance.

Think the thoughts that you have and feel the feelings that you have in this trance.

Staying in your favourite trance, it's time to open your eyes and see what the world looks like from this position. If you can, walk about a bit and notice what the world sounds like from this trance position. And how does it all feel?

Take a further few minutes to get to know even more what being in this trance is like for you.

Now... very vigorously and quickly, with freedom of movement for all your limbs, jump up and down on the spot 10 times.

Notice how AWAKE and alive this makes you. Notice how clear your head is. Notice how your passion and power are immediately coursing through your veins.

Where's your deadening trance gone???

Did you know you could change your state and connect with outtayerbox YOU that easily?

Well, now you do...

Congratulations... Excellently done!

And, of course, I know this exercise might not be the most appropriate thing to do in your appraisal meeting or the team 'catch-up' time, although the mischievous part of me wants to dare you to do it anyway. Less obvious alternatives to wake yourself up are slapping both cheeks of your face at the same time or pinching yourself very hard in a vulnerable, soft spot on your body.

If you have the privacy of your own office, do your jumping up and down there. Or in a cubicle in your staff toilets when no-one else's around. If someone catches you, you could always say you are energising yourself which is absolutely true. You are!

Be inventive! Find places where you can use this 20 second exercise to change from your unproductive and trance spin on your world to your awake and outtayerbox YOU.

The more you practise whacking yourself out of trances, the more you'll reinforce and embed your new awake behaviour. Until, eventually, you don't need to jump up and down at all. You'll have created being awake and identifying with outtayerbox YOU as a habit. And it will become as second nature to you as brushing your teeth.

In the meantime, you can also have a bit of fun. Because there are many ways you can start getting outtayerbox. Here's an essential one...

> Pretend you're a scientist studying yourself and
> that you're carrying out a crucially important
> experiment... which you are.

It's an experiment to become familiar with your out of sync experiences so that you learn how to recognise and use them creatively... AND how to connect with your inner leader, with outtayerbox YOU.

Carry a small notebook with you at all times. Record in it your thoughts, feelings, sensations and anything else you notice about yourself at times when you 'feel' out of sync. At times when you sense something's just not right even if you don't know what it is.

To begin with, just write your impressions about what you're seeing, hearing, saying, doing, thinking and feeling.

Like... 'Received the latest policy statement in this morning's meeting with a smile although I don't like what it says.'

In that moment, or later, note the details of your incongruence. How precisely is this policy not in line with your beliefs and values? What in it offends you?

Another first impression could be... 'Part of me wanted to shout GET ON WITH IT at the meeting this morning.'

What was the feeling under that desire to shout out? What were you registering at that meeting, perhaps like the child in The Emperor's New Clothes, which made you feel that way?

As you build up the muscle of connection inside and outside yourself with outtayerbox YOU you'll more rapidly and consciously understand what's going on. And, as you do, you'll begin to discover you have choices in how you think, feel and behave.

For example, once you know what's going on with you, you could choose to be honest in voicing your concerns about that policy. Then you could choose to offer suggestions for improvement. Or not. Your choice.

What? It doesn't come within your sphere of influence to make creative suggestions in line with your deepest integrity? Who says? Only 'convention'. Some employers and line managers enjoy their direct reports going the extra mile. Or not. The choice is up to you.

For example, once you know what's going on with you, you could choose to assert in the meeting, encouraging people to get back on point. Or not. Your choice.

What? You're not 'the chair'. So what?

If the chair's not doing their job, wasting the time and energy of attendees and the organisation's money, a respectful nudge from you in the direction of economy makes a gift to everyone there. Or not. It's up to you.

And, if your answer to these examples is NOT, then use your inner leader, your outtayerbox YOU, to manage your uncomfortable feelings.

For example, I'm not happy about this policy statement and, as I'm not going to do anything about it, time to let it go... AND MOVE ON!

For example, I'm frustrated by the lack of direction in this meeting and, as I'm not going to do anything about it, time to let my frustration go. Chill baby chill... AND MOVE ON!

The more you do your experimenting, recognising, understanding, connecting with YOU, making clear choices and managing your state (instead of being unhappy or seething with nowhere to go) the more you'll get to know how you tick... and how you CAN tick as a person.

You'll learn what's important for you, what's not, and what you need to be and do and have to experience your purpose, passion and power at work.

So, how could you start behaving more in line with outtayerbox YOU right now at work?

No excuses!

Anything but anything within your sphere of influence *and* out of it can be changed. Your sphere of influence is far more vast than you could ever imagine. Both outside yourself AND within!

Because reality is, while you can't change anyone else, and ultimately you might not be able to change the circumstances, you can always, always change yourself. Rather than reacting, you can always, always, choose how you experience what's going on and how you respond to it!

CHAPTER 8 – PURPOSE
IS IT A BIRD, IS IT A 'PLANE, IS IT.... ?

'Find out who you are and do it on purpose.'
Dolly Parton

So what is a 'purpose'?

For a start, it has nothing to do with a 'should', 'must' or 'have to'. There are enough people in the world kidding themselves that the noble cause they're following is their purpose when it's just something they thought they 'ought' to do.

It's also not a 'thing' like 'climbing Mount Everest.' Your purpose is never ever something to do.

Quite the opposite! Your purpose is your personal theme, your own particular signature tune.

I worked with a female executive who was on sick leave because she'd hit a crisis of meaning and slipped into depression. You know the one. It goes, 'What on earth is life all about. This can't be all there is!'

She'd left an unsatisfying job some months ago for another which seemed to hold the promise of so much more. Only, once she changed jobs, a swift reorganisation changed her job spec and she found herself once more, or so it seemed, in an unsatisfying position.

A not unfamiliar story in changing times. However, the double blow did it for her and brought her low.

That was her whack around the head. The Universe knocked her door flat and absolutely demolished it to let the hurricanes through.

When I first met this client, she just couldn't see her way forward. By the time we'd reached her third session she was beginning to recapture some of her vitality and enthusiasm. But the 'dreaded' job still loomed like the harbinger of doom.

During our work that day I asked her what her purpose was. The word 'dancing' popped out of her mouth without hesitation. "What a fabulous purpose to have," I said. "Dancing through life for yourself and others!" She positively glowed. Then, she frowned heavily. "But that's not much. That can't be my purpose!"

She'd made the #1 mistake most people do which makes finding your purpose a difficult, arduous and elusive task.

You expect you're going to discover your purpose with the London Philharmonic Orchestra stridently performing the 1812 Overture or at least a royal trumpet accolade from H.R.H.'s personal musicians. And you expect that your purpose will be similarly dramatic.

"Your purpose isn't that much?!" I replied. "I can't think of a more wonderful thing to be doing. The world needs people like you who can dance through life and show others the way to do it too."

It was if city centre Christmas lights had just been switched on, as she finally appreciated the value of her purpose for her own well-being and that of others.

Once she'd 'got' it, we talked about the many ways in which she could express her purpose at work. For her that was through humour, lightness and seeing how she could influence through her job by helping other people to 'dance'.

Reality is that there are an infinite number of ways you can manifest your purpose. It all depends on what you understand your purpose to be and the things which will fulfil both it *and* bring you enjoyment.

Finding and living your purpose was not meant to be a struggle and misery!

Once my client found the ways in which she wanted to express her purpose at work, it stopped being the 'dreaded' job. She became eager to return and experiment with her new knowledge and learning. And, surprise, surprise, when she did, she discovered her position was no longer unsatisfying even though nothing about it had changed while she'd been away.

That doesn't mean she'll be there forever or in time she won't seek a higher position or do something else entirely. What it *does* mean is, by finding her purpose and living it, she turned her job around from dissatisfying to enjoyable.

And, by living in the now, she developed life skills she could take forward into whatever future work her career held in store.

It's important you realise that your purpose will express itself whatever the nature of your current situation, and whether you're aware of it or not.

It's part of what I call your 'oomph', your essential life energy. Whether you listen to it or not, whether you invite the Universe to knock your door down or not, whether you're conscious of it or not, it will be appearing in your life somewhere, right now... even if you don't consciously recognise it.

Because your purpose has a compelling urge to be turned into real life action. And, as it can do that in an infinite number of ways, it will use whatever means it has at its disposal.

So here are further excavations to loosen up your purpose finding muscles. And please, please don't give answers to fool yourself. Stick with your authentic answers, however uncomfortable they might be.

Are you doing that hobby because you love doing it or was it the 'appropriate' thing to do? Are the people you socialise with really the kind of people who float your boat? Or did you just fall in with that crowd? Or were they your partner's friends? Are you doing your current job because it inspired you? Or did you just fall into that too?

How arrogant of me! Of course you can fool yourself if you like. Who am I to stop you? But I'm sure you know the maxim 'garbage in, garbage out'. I rest my case...

> What part of your job do you enjoy most of all?
> What hobbies, if any, do you enjoy?

What do you love doing in your leisure time?

And I do mean LOVE... not 'like' but unadulterated LOVE!

What kind of music do you enjoy the most?
If you weren't human, what animal would you love to be?
What kind of people do you love socialising with most?
Which is the country you would most love to visit?

Put your answers away for 24 hours. Then read them again and notice the common theme which runs through most of your answers.

Make a note of it. If there isn't 'a' theme, it's probably because there's more than one. So make a note of them.

And then, ask yourself, what's the meta, higher order, or common theme which joins them altogether?

It won't be a bird. It won't be a 'plane. And it won't be you as Super Man or Woman. Remember, your purpose is never a 'thing' and always a theme, your signature tune.

Listen!

I can almost hear your purpose melodically playing itself already...

CHAPTER 9 – PURPOSE AT WORK???

'Winners are people with definite purpose in life.'
Denis Waitley

If you've tried it, it's likely that talking about your 'purpose' at work wasn't received as a very 'organisational' or acceptable thing to do. What rubbish.

It's perfectly acceptable to speak about the organisation's values or mission statement but this is often so much token talk. The statement can often lay curling in someone's desk while 'the way things have always been done around here' continues unchecked. Without sensitive and consistent handling, the pre-existent work culture wins out every time.

If your personal purpose is considered at all it's in an 'all in together folks, singing from the same hymn sheet' kind of way. The assumption is made that the organisation's mission statement is of course *your* mission statement. If it's not, then HR gets involved to work out how they can get you 'to come on board'.

How crazy! This is butt about face.

The way for great staff engagement and retention is to help you discover your own purpose and, then, how your outtayerbox YOU and it can be married with the organisational purpose.

Then you'd be assigned to a role which would generally enthuse you and you'd become more effective and productive as a result. Of course, there are always things about any job you'd not be keen about. But they'd pale into insignificance given your general enjoyment at work.

Your purpose is powerful. It's far too important to be organisationally overlooked.

I think of my purpose as both my highest principle and the very foundation from which I operate in the world. It's both things at the same time although I know that sounds paradoxical. But it's not either one or the other. It's simultaneously both together.

My purpose informs me and gives meaning to what I do, while what I do reflects back to me my purpose and the nature of my being. So my purpose is both my guiding star and the rock which supports me. It's the signature tune of my life.

And, while the words of my purpose have changed over time, as will yours, its central theme remains constant; one of service for the growth of myself and others.

Phew! Feel a bit shy, gauche and tearful at remembering my purpose. Not unlike how many of my clients react when they've searched for something more in their lives and discovered the something more is within. And not the things they were chasing outside of their selves. You know the story. Better car, bigger house, more expensive holiday... and the rest.

Paradoxically, again, their discoveries came from our conversations about *not* having purpose or meaning. They came from starting points like an imposed change at work, general dissatisfaction, feeling inadequate or things not living up to expectations.

I recently worked with a retail operation's executive in his mid 40s who was bitterly disappointed with how his career had gone. Out of our continuing conversations he realised he'd been carrying his parents' expectations about what career achievements he 'should have made by his 40s' instead of what was true for him.

More was to come. For, when he discovered his purpose, he was delighted to realise the career level he'd achieved gave him stimulating work which was in line with how he wanted to express it. He could make a particular difference in his existing role for the betterment of his own, and other people's lives, that he was inspired to by his purpose.

Actually, the secret is that it never matters what job you're doing or what position you hold. *Whatever* your purpose, it can always, always be turned into action through your current job. So my client's realisation can be your realisation too.

He didn't need to be an executive director to be successful or fulfil his purpose. He could do all of that exactly where he was in his career right now. And, in fact, he realised he was playing an even bigger game than the career one.

Can you imagine what that awareness did for his general emotional, physical and psychological health? What would it do for yours and for the quality of *your* life and relationships?

A little while later my client saw that his purpose could be even better fulfilled in another area of the company's operation. On fire with the passion and power which comes from being connected to your purpose, he made an excellent business case for the transfer and got it.

None of this took away the chance he had to develop himself into executive director or CEO material if he wanted. In fact, it helped him realise that he had a choice to do that or not. He no longer experienced himself as a failure without opportunity as he'd done when we started working together.

> Think about your work situation.
>
> How well does your organisation's mission statement fit with you? ... assuming you know what it is? What do you think of it? How do you feel about it?
>
> If there is a mismatch between what you think and what you feel about your organisation's mission statement, what's that about?
>
> If you can't find words to describe the mismatch, choose a symbol, like a colour or a person or an object, to represent that difference.
>
> And what do all your answers tell you about your own purpose?
>
> Hold that thought!

It seems to me there's a 'push' with growing momentum that's a kind of 'looking-for-something-more' human virus. While plenty of people are happy with or resigned to go along with how things are at work, I come across many in my professional role who feel the discomfort of their outtayerbox YOU knocking at their door.

Some have described it to me as an urge for more than their usual personal identity, positions and posturing. How delicious! Wanting to be more than the emperor with or, more correctly, without his new clothes.

The tasty thing about discovering your purpose and having a sense of being on a bigger endeavour or adventure which is not just work, yet includes work, is it encourages you to...

Be response-able!

This is not the heavy duty 'responsibility' thing which you've probably been taught is a burden, a chain and ball which keeps you controlled. This 'response-ability' is the skill to make choices relevant to the situational moment you're in rather than react from old patterns of behaviour.

Scenario... Boss is irritable and snaps at you. Not OK but it happens. Old pattern of behaviour, the 'reaction', could be to imagine you've done something wrong to upset your boss and to start worrying what that could be.

Alternatively, your 'response', rather than a reaction, could be to note your boss's irritation in the moment. Then let it go instead of getting wound up. And, at a time when your boss would be open to feedback, you could choose to give it along with an encouragement to address you without snapping.

Live in line with your purpose!

When you do, you start feeling you don't want to do things that aren't in line with your purpose. And you develop a preference for doing things which are.

Scenario... You're invited to a departmental social event. You know the people organising it. They've done it before and you know what kind of event it will be. In the past you went along and suffered it to be one of the 'boys' or one of the 'girls'.

Living in line with your purpose could be appreciating your invitation and declining it with a simple "I'm unable to come this time". Or, because it is important politically for you to be there, you could attend accepting it for what it is without an emotional charge. This would enable you to take enjoyment from moments which *are* in line with your purpose.

Have a willingness to live in the world just as it is!

And that doesn't mean you deny possibilities for improvements to 'what is' or even work to achieve them. It just means acceptance of what's going on now without having to get all steamed up about it.

Have a sense of destiny and a meaning to live!

This is not about fate, or having your life pre-determined. This sense of destiny is about having an over-arching mission to achieve in life and choosing it through the different paths you take.

If anyone had told me thirty years ago I would be doing the work I'm doing and sitting here writing this book, I wouldn't have believed them. Yet, when I look back and see the choices I made or didn't make, the different avenues I explored and chose not to, it's not hard to see how I arrived at this point.

What about you?

When I first came across this stuff I thought, "WOW... WHO? *ME*!?" It looked too big and sounded and felt too grand for me. And that really was so much reverse snobbery; that it was OK for other more worthy people but not for me.

I learned my 'WHO? *ME*!?' reaction was the workings of what I call my 'gremlins'. Just like that executive in the retail operation, you and I have heard a load of outmoded ideas, attitudes, beliefs and behaviours which we learned from our family, schools, friends and other organisations growing up... and beyond.

These are your gremlins, the ones which want to keep you as cannon fodder or robotic cogs in the wheel of the world at work. The ones that want you to stay exactly as you are. Don't upset the apple-cart or rock the boat whatever you do.

Some would say if it works don't fix it. But does it work for you?

Do the gremlins' messages leave you fulfilled in who you are and what you do? And for whom *exactly* do the gremlins work? Because I'm pretty sure they're not working for the benefit of outtayerbox YOU.

If you've already become aware of your purpose, you'll know the experience of expandedness, of deeply felt engagement and purposeful action for your own and the higher good. And if you've not become aware of your purpose that might sound like so much high falutin' mumbo-jumbo! Or maybe not.

Your purpose is right in front of your nose. It's just a hair's breadth away. And whatever it is, once known, you, your work and your life will never ever be the same again... even if it is!

> Close your eyes, take a deep breath and imagine your purpose at the end of your nose, just a hair's breadth away.

> That might sound silly to your logical mind. If it does, tell it the ancient Greek origins of the word 'silly' meant blessed, happy and blissful. So yes... very silly!

> And, if your logical mind just revolted, thank it for being so sensible. Then assure it that, once you access other types of intelligence, your mind will have so much more information with which to discover your purpose.

> So... Close your eyes, take a deep breath and imagine your purpose is actually at the end of your nose, just a hair's breadth away. You could get a picture, a sense of something, sensations in your body, sounds...anything! Take whatever you get however bizarre.

Jot down what you got in words or pictures or scribbles and then walk away from it. Leave it alone while your unconscious, both logical and illogical, works with the information you've got so far.

And in the hours and days ahead be prepared for the insights and realisations which will occur to you. Make sure you have that notebook of yours to record what you discover. A curious feature of an AHA! is you can forget it as quickly as it came.

So be warned! Jot down your insights and realisations about your purpose right there at the end of your nose as soon as you get them.

And remember, being who you are, where you are and doing exactly what you're doing is absolutely the right place for you to find your purpose at work right now!

CHAPTER 10 – Purpose
Living dangerously!

'All serious daring starts from within.'

Eudora Welty

I had a conversation with a colleague in Cumbria last night. We were discussing living our respective passions, what stirs us, what excites us, what pulls us onward whether we know it consciously or not.

And these words are paltry compared with the sensational inside YEEESSSSS! you feel when you're on track with yourself and your purpose. There is no vocabulary to describe this or the certain uncertainty which accompanies you when you tread a path you've not trod before... yet you know THIS IS IT!

Our conversation also reminded me of the many times I've said NO to my purpose's urging. Those times when it caught my attention and tugged at me to follow a signpost which I didn't understand or know precisely where it was going.

It also reminded me of the times when I've raised my eyes to the sky, and still do, yelling, "Haven't I done enough already?"

The answer is of course 'No!'... Because your purpose unfolds and develops just as you unfold and develop as a person.

Remember, your purpose is a theme and not an action. And the ways in which you can express your purpose change over time, just as you change and grow. So, there is always the possibility of something else to be doing... which, of course, can be exciting. It can also be more than just a bit scary too!

But that's far more favourable than 'living dead', sticking to doing what's expected of you or doing the opposite as a rebellion against all you've been taught which you mistake for asserting your free will. And it's far more favourable than being in the pain of that restlessness or frustration which says you're missing out somehow.

If you sit very quietly you might just hear your own restlessness, a symptom of your own purpose, calling out exactly what you're missing. Even if you don't consciously know what that is right now.

What you might tell yourself, or other people might tell you, is this is all indulgent nonsense. Navel gazing! Just get your head down and keep doing what you've always done, getting the results you've always got. Yet that's an act of insanity if you want life to be different.

When I wanted to study a degree, my ex husband told me I should have thought of doing that *before* I got married. Derrr! AND that's one kind of excuse you can give yourself to not listen to your purpose...

That it's too late, it's not the right time. As if there's ever a right time. You and only you can *make* it the right time.

Other excuses not to listen to your purpose can be about 'who do you think you are to be different?' and other 'I can't do that' gremlins.

Even when you consciously know your purpose, you can still trick yourself by using the same old same old bedraggled excuses. I know because, even now, I still hear my gremlins at times doing it to me, nagging away at me with their rubbish.

And if you choose not to be influenced by them it means you start to live deliciously dangerously. It means you start moving from the point where you are in your life to who knows where you might end up.

Or as a client I worked with said, "I didn't know life could be so good without me changing a damn thing except myself!"

Living dangerously doesn't mean risking your life, throwing in your career or job... unless of course you really want to. It doesn't mean walking away from everything you know and taking a boat up the Amazon or opening a soup kitchen... unless of course you really want to.

What living dangerously means is you don't have to be anything else that you're not already being, do anything else than you're not already doing or go anywhere else than where you already are. Your starting point is right now this moment if you choose to take the opportunity.

And the really good news is, if you don't take the opportunity in this moment, you can take it in the next, or the next, or the next...

Opportunity is always but always there for you to live dangerously, being wide awake and absolutely present with what's going on in your world moment by moment. Living dangerously is aligning yourself with your purpose and be-doing as only you can be and do... whatever that is.

There's a story told about the renowned psychiatrist and proponent of medical hypnosis, Milton Erickson and a particular person with whom he worked.

> A neighbour was worried about the woman next door who seemed to be severely depressed and wouldn't leave her house or see anyone. So, making a very persuasive and comprehensive argument, she got Dr Erickson to stop by. And she got her neighbour to accept a visit from the 'great man'.
>
> He came and was surprised at the squalor in which the woman lived which was beyond anything he'd seen before. However, he asked her to show him her house and she gladly complied impervious to the state of her surroundings.
>
> Dr Erickson didn't say a word as he was shown around, just quietly observed whatever there was to observe. In one of the rooms he noticed a dying African Violet. Clearly the flower was

suffering from as much neglect as the house and as the woman of herself as well.

But at the end of her showing him round, Dr Erickson said to the woman, "I noticed you had an African Violet and can tell you love flowers. So, here's what I want you to do..."

He told her to go out and buy some African Violet seeds and plant them in her backyard. He gently encouraged her to care for them and make sure they grew to beautiful flowers.

When they'd fully grown, he told her to buy a newspaper and search all the births, deaths and marriages in the neighbourhood. Each time she found one, she was to send the people concerned one of her beautiful African violets with a note to say they were from her. And he finished by asking if she could do that for him.

The woman eagerly agreed. She'd found a purpose in life. And, for years and years, she sent out her violets, giving herself and others great joy from her simple act. She became renowned in her city for being the mysterious woman who sent an African violet on those important occasions.

Many hundreds of people attended her funeral when she died to pay respect and to mourn the passing of a woman who'd come to be greatly loved. A woman simply known as the African Violet lady.

She could have stayed in her depressive stupor whatever Dr Erickson had said to her. She chose otherwise. She chose to live dangerously, to move from the point where she was into an unknown future. She chose to be inspired by her purpose and follow it through in a way she could easily do.

You too have a sense of the something you can do in the world, however, small or huge. Whether that's growing African Violets or nurturing your children or creating the next technological innovation or working for world peace... or all four. Who knows!

And, despite the scariness, I promise you'll feel so alive that it will be as if you've been reborn. You'll feel so alive trusting the 'not-knowing' when you don't. You'll feel so alive seeing how, little by little, your purpose reveals to you your passion and way forward... for now!

CHAPTER 11 – PURPOSE
WHAT THE...!

'Here is a test to find whether your mission on Earth is finished: If you're alive, it isn't.'
Richard Bach

After reading so far and doing the exercises, your mind, consciously or unconsciously, will be vibrating big time because of the varied information the exercises are designed to deliver. Hopefully, you will also have had some feelings and/or sensations.

If your feelings or experiences have been of the 'I can't be doing with this' kind... congratulations! You're exactly where you need to be.

If your feelings or experiences have been of the 'Wahoooo!' kind... congratulations! You're exactly where *you* need to be.

And, if you already have a sense or even know for sure what your purpose is... congratulations! You too are exactly where you need to be.

And, if you think this is all a load of baloney... congratulations! You are most definitely where *you* need to be.

And, if you have no idea about anything much any more... congratulations. You too are absolutely and most definitely where you need to be!

You've been loosening up the muscles of your emotional, sensory and intuitive intelligences, developing their connection with your logical mind and organic wisdom.

Your body has an inbuilt organic programme which always tries to renew and mend you physically when you're ill or have been injured. In the same way, your outtayerbox YOU always tries to move you psychologically to more 'wellness', to better health and integration.

Knowing your purpose is one of the ways it does that...

An eminent CEO was looking for his purpose and heard of an extremely wise teacher from a long dynasty of 'gurus' who it was said could teach the meaning of life. Now the CEO had read book after book, practised technique after technique, informed himself of all the latest articles, theories and general information about finding his purpose.

He was full up to the brim of himself with intellectual ideas yet his purpose eluded him. And he decided this wise teacher was the woman to see and the only person who could help him.

So, with his second in command in place, the CEO travelled half way round the world to get to the university campus from which the wise teacher worked. Having emailed her in advance, she'd already invited him to take tea with her on a certain date.

The allotted time and day arrived. The eminent CEO could not contain himself with excitement. On meeting the wise teacher, he was overcome with his desire to find his purpose and strove to impress her with his worthiness. He showered her with all his knowledge on the subject from his many years of intellectual study.

There was a long silence during which he suddenly feared he'd gone too far and had offended the wise teacher in some way. But no. At last she smiled, having taken time to reflect on how best to teach this impatient prospective student. "My friend," she said, as was customary in her country, "... before all that, let's have some tea."

Her secretary brought in a pot of tea with two cups ready and placed the tray in front of them on a glass coffee table. The wise teacher leaned forward, took the pot and begun pouring tea into the CEO's cup.

She poured and poured until the golden liquid spilled over the cup's edges. Then, it cascaded over the saucer's edges and on to the table until the CEO just had to remonstrate with the wise teacher about exactly what she thought she was doing.

She stopped pouring the golden fountain.

As the pool spread slowly over the glass she remarked, "My friend, you are like this cup overfull with knowledge about what you seek. If you want to discover the true meaning of your life, you must first empty your cup of knowledge to allow room for the new and different to pour in."

Some of the previous exercises will have done some of that for you, encouraging ways of thinking that you can't get from articles, books and theories. Some of the previous exercises were limbering up your intelligences and connections with your outtayerbox YOU and its inherent, organic knowledge.

So... What next?

Whether you think you know your purpose or not, whether you think you don't or whether you think this is a pile of hooey, given all your previous work, the next exercise can take you to your purpose in life. The more open you are the sooner you'll reach it and the less open you are the longer it will take.

That's all!

Where ever you are in the process of discovery, this exercise can successfully give you your purpose one way or another.

Use a blank sheet of paper and hand write or use a blank document file on your PC, whichever method is the most attractive to you right now.

At the top of the paper or file write...

My purpose in life is...

Line by line, finish the sentence. Record it using the first answer which pops into your head. For example, My purpose in life is... eating rhubarb.

By now you'll be used to writing down the bizarre things you get or converting pictures you get into words. My only plea is for you to record the very first answer which comes. Whether that's a whole sentence, a short phrase or one word. Whatever you get is 100% correct.

Keep repeating the statement, 'My purpose in life is...' and write your answers one line after another on your paper/file speedily and without consideration. Just write whatever comes, however peculiar.

Repeat doing this until you write an answer from which you immediately get a very, very big or huge emotional response. That's your purpose!

And if it seems nonsensical to you, just accept it. Over the hours and days to come your statement will fall into place and you'll know exactly what your purpose is.

While this is the essence of the exercise, read the rest of the chapter before you begin it.

How long will it take you? Well, it depends not just on how open or not you are. It also depends on how much you've limbered up and how much cup emptying you've done.

What's important is to do it without interruptions and just keep going and going at it. The time you feel you most want to give up is precisely the time to keep going.

It means you're right on track and the gremlins don't like it too much. So keep going. The desire to stop will then soon pass.

I know that life happens. Sometimes you have to take care of the children unexpectedly, take emergency action over a stranded friend or rescue a cat from a tree.

If, for any important reason, a lengthy break is necessary, just accept the intervention. When you're next able, return to the exercise, read what you wrote before, each sentence beginning with the headline, and then re-start where you left off.

You'll find that some of your answers will repeat themselves or be very similar to previous answers. No matter. Keep going.

You might also get answers which give you a small surge of feeling but you don't get a 'whammeee'. This means those answers are more on track than others but don't labour them. Just highlight them in some way so you can come back to them when you get an urge to do so... and you might discover new variations on that theme.

If you feel the need to take a break, close your eyes and be still for a moment. As you do, focus your attention on the intention that your answers come as easily and elegantly as they surely will.

When you find THE answer, your own unique answer to what your purpose is, you'll get a strong reaction. A veritable whack around the head.

You could find yourself experiencing an enormous gob-smack or a 'bloody 'ell'. You could cry deeply and be smiling at the same time. You could feel very jubilant. You could explode with an internal high five. And for some people it could be a deep non-verbal recognition of '*YES!... THIS IS IT!*'

Whatever your reaction, the words that you've written for your purpose will have a powerful energy way beyond the words themselves.

Even though I know the theme of my purpose, I decided to do this exercise again so I could re-experience and talk authentically with you about it. And, although I'm pretty clued up, it took me 35 minutes to get to my 'hot' answer. So it might or might not take you a lot more.

Some phrases which came near the beginning of my list had me reacting with tears pricking the back of my eyes. And then... nothing!

By answer #30 I thought, "This is tedious! I know what my purpose is anyway so what on earth am I doing this for?" But I kept going and kept going, mindful of the gremlins doing their stuff to stop me, until answer #44 hit me like a two ton truck!

And the addition of one word in what I thought my purpose was gave me the best whack around the head I've had for a long time. (Yes... me too!)

It was a call for me to be even *more* present, in the now, and with what I have to say. And it came through the addition of one word, but what a word...

Leading *fearlessly* with purpose, passion and power!

Remember, as your purpose grows and develops so do you. And as you grow and develop so does your purpose in how it wants to be expressed in the world. Although its theme always, always, remains the same, the words can change over time, even completely.

So, stick with the exercise, however long it takes you and however many answers you write. Censor nothing. Criticise nothing. Negate nothing. Everything plays its part in the journey of discovering your purpose right now!

CAUTION 1

Once you discover your purpose and leave it a day or two it can all feel like an anti-climax. "So what! I know what my purpose is *AND*...???" If that happens in less than a day or two, you're really humming.

You might get a desire to ignore your purpose. This is the gremlins at work, either exterior ones like unempathetic people in your life or internal ones from your own personality.

'Oh it all seems so much airy fairy stuff.' Or it all 'seems too hard.' 'Just carry on like normal... It'll be alright.'

That's all just part of your urge to keep yourself small and be indistinguishable from the herd. Fine if that's really how you want to be but that's all excuses not to stretch yourself. It's all just part of your 'shtick'!

CAUTION 2

And, if by now you haven't discovered or got a good sense of your purpose, that's probably also down to your 'shtick.'

CHAPTER 12
WHAT'S YOUR SHTICK?

'Don't tell fish stories where the people know you; but particularly, don't tell them where they know the fish.'

Mark Twain

'Shtick' comes from Yiddish, a once traditional 'second language' of Eastern European Jewish communities so they could communicate across countries. Very important when you were likely to be exiled at a moment's notice and needing to find help somewhere else.

A shtick originally meant a comic theme or theatrical gimmick which later came to mean a repeated performance or routine. And finally led to meaning your 'story'.

Please remember your shtick is meat and drink to your negative gremlins.

Long ago when I was restless and getting very minor whacks around the head, my shtick, repeated story and behaviour, was to say that I couldn't do anything because my husband wouldn't like it. Sound familiar?

In truth, my then husband didn't like me doing anything out of the ordinary routine *and* that didn't mean I was powerless. I just acted so. And, of course, through acting as if I was powerless, nothing happened. Nothing changed.

So, remember that your shtick is very powerful. What you think, what you believe and tell yourself, your story, then, as if by magic, creates your reality!

'I have to stay in this job because of the money...' Guess what experience of the job that creates.

'I know I could do so much better *but*...' Notice how the 'but' creates a spurious reason for not doing better, whatever the excuse.

'*If only* I'd got that promotion...' says 'I'm defeated before I even start.' What a great motivator!

'I'll *try* to make that project more inspiring...' You either do something or you don't do something. 'Try' is wishy-washy. It's got failure built in and, worse still, invites it.

You programme your brain through what you think and what language you use. There's a part of it called the Reticular Activating System thought to be highly involved in attention and motivation which is also highly susceptible to our thoughts and language.

Just bought a superb silver monster of a car? Then what happens? You see hundreds of other superb silver monsters of the same make on every route you drive.

That's because your attention and motivation is aroused to notice other superb silver monsters because superb silver monsters are absolutely at the top of your pile of thoughts... having just bought one!

I worked with a manager who'd been made redundant. The redundancy hadn't been handled well by the organisation and she was left feeling totally de-skilled and inadequate. 'I'm useless' was her shtick. Not a good frame of mind in which to make decisions about your future career.

Anyhow, I knew she felt disillusioned by corporate life and was considering starting her own business. And when I saw her next she told me about a card selling operation somebody had recommended to her.

On examination it certainly looked like pyramid selling with the people at the bottom doing all the work and getting a pittance per unit as profit. Plus she was vastly over qualified for the tasks the job entailed.

She wriggled at my questioning and disliked my challenges about how she was undermining and underselling herself to herself let alone to anyone else. And then the lights went on!

Her confident self wouldn't have dreamed of such an enterprise. It was totally out of line with her purpose. And, once she realised this and that she wasn't useless but in distress, the card selling scheme was dropped quickly like a hot lump of elephant dung.

You'll find you usually have more than one shtick. Discovering what they are is invaluable.

Once you know your excuse stories for not being as magnificent as you can be, for not following your purpose, you can do something neutralising about them. But first you've got to identify what it or they are.

This is crucial work.

This determines whether you take your purpose forward and engage your passion and your power in your work right now. Or whether you do same old same old.

Do the next exercise all in one go and leave a substantial amount of time to complete it. If that's not possible, complete one section at a time. However, it's important to do the whole thing on the same day. You'll lose essential threads if you do it over time and take too long. So be warned!

Create a list of your shticks, the excuses you give yourself for not being and doing what you truly desire to be and do.

Do it on the left hand side of an A3 sheet or 2 pieces of A4 cello-taped together. Divide into 4 columns. Leave a line between each entry.

Knowing your purpose will help you in the exercise as you can explore the shticks which are going 'SO WHAT!' in your head and the reasons they give you for not following your purpose.

In the left hand column put in the header...

MY SHTICKS ARE...

For example...

I'm too old for this.

I'm not good enough for this?

Who do I think I am to be growing ideas?

I can't save the world because it's my turn to cook dinner...

OK... I know that last one's jokey. Or is it? What are the shticks you've created about the ordinary actions of your life, like cooking dinner or going to the gym, which give you an excuse NOT to work in line with your purpose?

Write your list now in Column 1 and keep going until you're totally 'cooked'.

And what's the price you pay for each of your shticks?

I once knew of someone who was medically retired in his early 50s from a managerial position due to his psychological inability to cope with 'too much' stress. Instead of seeking professional help to develop better coping strategies and techniques, he chose to retire to a 'quiet life' where he wouldn't be challenged to cope with much.

Life events of course happened as they do, but a mixture of anti-depressants and comatose-by-television saw him through. He often told me he was quite contented with his life. Yet, he seemed to fall asleep regularly on and off during the day. I suspect his 'contentment' was boredom in drag.

Choices, choices, choices! And the price of his shtick, 'I can't cope with too much stress', was the deterioration of a lively mind and eventually, due to lack of activity, turning himself into a semi-invalid.

I'd have chosen the professional help any day!

In Column 2 write the header...

THE PRICE I PAY FOR THIS SHTICK

And fill it in going through your shticks one by one.

For example...

MY SHTICKS ARE	THE PRICE I PAY FOR THIS SHTICK
I'm too old for this.	I miss opportunities to learn new things.
I'm not good enough for this.	I hold myself back.
Who do I think I am to be growing ideas?	I deny myself adventures.
I can't save the world because it's my turn to cook dinner.	I get frustrated by things I have to do.

How do you get your rocks off with your shticks, the little pockets of drama you create to stop yourself

110

fulfilling your purpose? Sounds harsh of me? You bet it's harsh of me!

You've only got this one life, as far as I know, and living other people's ideas and other people's lives instead of your own seems a total waste to me.

So own up!

For example, that medical retiree? Well, I guess the idea of getting his rocks off with his shtick wouldn't occur to him at all. But your shticks always develop without you consciously knowing and for a very good reason at the time.

For example, that medical retiree could have had a parent or loved one who, in the past, experienced a mental breakdown through being over-stressed. So, in a curious and unconscious way, he could have been protecting himself from the fear of a breakdown happening to him by telling himself retiring was the only way to make sure he didn't go 'crazy' too.

'Phew... What a relief. I won't chance that one now!'

He could have felt inadequate and, as the job got more demanding, he could have feared being found out as a 'fraud'. That's not an uncommon fear amongst people in organisations.

So, 'Phew... What a relief. I won't now chance that one either!'

He could have been just plain old fearful of the unknown. There haven't been any jobs for life with safe pensions for at least 20 years now.

So, 'Phew... What a relief. I won't chance losing my job. I'll organise my own 'chop' instead before anyone else does.'

The source of getting your rocks off through your shtick usually relates to relief from a fear of some kind, even if it's fear of something very positive. Time for you to discover what your fear or fears are. The bogey man always shrinks in size when you see him in daylight!

Head up the third column with...

ROCKS OFF...

You'll see below that, as I can't get more than two headings sensibly on one of these pages, I've laid them out in column form.

Your exercise sheet will show the three columns horizontally. And each answer to MY SHTICKS ARE, PRICE I PAY and ROCKS OFF will follow through, 1 to 1 and 2 to 2, etc., as they did in the last worked example.

MY SHTICKS ARE
1. I'm too old for this.
2. I'm not good enough for this.

PRICE I PAY
1. I miss opportunities to learn new things.
2. I hold myself back.

ROCKS OFF
1. I play it safe to avoid the fear of looking stupid. Phew!
2. I don't have to risk failing. Phew!

You know the rest. Go to it!

And, if you want to stop, just know it's the gremlins not wanting you to know even more about your shtick.

Knowledge is power, as you will see.

Now you know the price you pay for your shtick and how it helps you get your rocks off. This, strangely enough, is also its positive intention for you. Its 'positive intention' is what it's trying to 'do good' for you, like protecting you from your fear of looking stupid.

Because maybe you were made to feel stupid at some time in your life. And it was so painful that you unconsciously decided you wouldn't risk going anywhere near that experience again. In that case, there's nothing like a good shtick to keep you away from anything but anything, however small, which might chance you repeating the experience.

So, now you've discovered some of the stories you tell yourself to hold back from being as big and as magnificent as you can be.

You've discovered what you say to yourself, what the result of what you say to yourself is and what it's doing for you. Now you know all that, here comes the fun part.

Imagine you are the worst kind of actor or actress. Go down your list of shticks and say each one of them out loud, hamming them up horribly wonderfully. Do it like a silent movie star with widening of eyes and exaggerated gestures. Do it in front of a mirror so you get the full Monty of your shtick.

And enjoy the drama! Enjoy how deliciously ludicrous your shtick is when you hear it and see it writ large. Truly magnificent in its own right!

Let your energy rip and enjoy the absurdity of the stories you tell yourself to stop you living your purpose. And, incidentally, they're the self same stories you tell yourself to keep you *inyerbox* and so much smaller than you really are.

Indeed, they're the stories you tell yourself to keep you from being the magnificence of outtayerbox YOU.

Enough! Here's the finale...

Go back to your lists and in the fourth column write...

MY NEW SHTICK

Your old stories were developed through your experiences. Some of them came from what you were told you were, how other people perceived your behaviour and what they said about you. 'Show off!' 'You'll come to nothing.' 'Bla-bla-bla-bla-bla.'

And, some came from unconscious decisions you made about life and how to navigate it. 'I need to hold myself back otherwise I get told off and hurt inside.' 'I mustn't outshine my sister, my brother, my father, my mother, the family dog....' 'Bla-bla-bla-bla-bla.'

But once you know your shtick, the price it makes you pay and its positive intention you can create new and totally effective shticks to get the most out of life.

> Head your fourth column MY NEW SHTICK and write the new story you want in your life, turning the old shtick around into a positive. Use key words from THE PRICE I PAY and ROCKS OFF to help you...
>
> MY SHTICKS ARE
> I'm too old for this.
>
> PRICE I PAY
> I miss opportunities to learn new things.
>
> ROCKS OFF
> I play it safe to avoid the fear of looking stupid.
>
> NEW SHTICK
> I am absolutely safe and take opportunities to learn new things.
>
> Now you 'take opportunities to learn' instead of 'missing opportunities to learn', don't you? And you are 'absolutely safe' whether you feel you look stupid or not, aren't you?
>
> As a final act, go through your list and put a big black thick line through every one of your old shticks.

They're your past. They're not your present or your future. End of!

Stand tall and relaxed, your list in front of you, and read out loud the new 'stories' you're telling yourself one by one. Say them in a confident and strong voice.

Notice how you feel as you read each of your new stories. Notice how you feel when you've finished the list.

Leave a minute's silence standing still... so you can really take in all your achievements, your new creative and supportive shticks.

You've reframed your old inhibiting ones. You've turned them from negative and limiting beliefs into positive and creative beliefs full of potential. So, make a fresh list only of your positive shticks and read them out loud every day.

Photocopy your list and put it in places where you'll often see your new shticks so they repeatedly reinforce and support your new behaviours.

You could put them on the fridge door. The back of a toilet door works well too. Have your list in a drawer you often pull out. Have them pinned to a computer screen if you're OK with that. And, generally, keep the list in your wallet or bag so you can regularly access it and read it to yourself to reinforce your new ways of being.

If you learned your times tables by rote you'll know the value of repetition repetition repetition.

Years ago, when I took a leap of faith leaving a relatively secure job for the world of self-employment, all my old insecurity shticks came into play. I feared I would lose everything and end up a bag lady, out on the streets with no-one to care about me.

Any time you stress yourself with a new challenge there's a chance the gremlins associated with your old shticks will come out to play to terrify you. So, always have your list to hand to remind yourself of the way things are... and just watch those gremlins deflate and disappear.

Anyhow, I did exactly the exercise you've just done when I had my fearful experience.

What's my shtick, what's the price I pay for having it and how do I get my rocks off through having it? Then, what's the new story I want to carry forward in my life? Mine, at the time, was 'I am absolutely safe and more than able to be successfully self-employed'.

Changing your thoughts changes your feelings. Changing them both changes the energy you put out in your workplace and your life. And changing the energy you put out dynamically changes the energy which comes towards you... even when it starts out not ideal. You now have an energy force field to neutralise it.

Congratulations!

You're now working from outtayerbox YOU in line with your purpose and things you previously thought were impossible have the opportunity to happen. They are now more than eminently possible!

CHAPTER 13
CHICKENS CAN'T FLY!

*'Flying is learning how to throw yourself
at the ground and miss.'*

Douglas Adams

An American friend, reared in a family of 12 who worked a small holding, fell about laughing when I told her I didn't know chickens could fly. "How come you don't know that?" she said. "Easy", I replied, "I've never seen one which can".

Oh, that old thing. Just because you don't see something in your life doesn't mean it doesn't exist.

Chickens are the most common birds on the planet with current estimates numbering them over 25 billion and growing. And, unless you were raised way out in the country where wild chickens roam, the only chickens you'll come across, if at all, are the domesticated kind wrapped in plastic!

So, you also might not have known that, in fact, chickens can fly. They fly to explore their surroundings. They fly to get away from potentially threatening events, like a fox or two. In fact, wild chickens can fly a fair distance and, for safety, up into the very top branches of trees.

No such luck for domesticated chickens. They usually have the tips of their longest feathers clipped on one wing to stop them flying away. This gives them a peculiar lopsided and drunken gait when they try to fly. You'll see them making an aborted lift off only for a couple of feet at the most.

Clipping their wings while stopping them from getting away also makes them far more susceptible to predators than their wild sisters. Pretty much the same as the difference between outtayerbox YOU and inyerbox you, I think.

Inyerbox you had your wings clipped by your growing up conditioning, your trances, gremlins and shticks. And, just like those farm-yard chickens, you've been force-fed with stuff to enhance the quality of 'food' you produce for the mass market. Unlike wild chickens who naturally eat a wide range of healthy foods, all of their own choosing.

That's your choice too. Be a domesticated chicken, all lopsided and with a funny gait. Or be one which can fly? Be a wild thing and let your heart sing...!

And that's all about cultivating self-belief, mixing with supportive people and taking one baby step at a time... or not... with Outtayerbox YOU.

If you don't believe in yourself, who will?

I've worked with some highly successful people who lacked self-belief. Sometimes they even felt amazed that they'd achieved so much. They put it down to a fluke, good luck or some other 'not them' factor. And they often had an underlying anxiety that one day they were going to be found out as a fraud.

A common way to cover up those underlying thoughts and feelings is bravado.

That was my own brand of corporate cover up. I looked confident. I talked confidently. I presented confidently. I would do things other people didn't have the gonads to do. Everybody thought I was excellent stuff when in reality I was sometimes a quivering wreck inside.

Bravado does a great cover up job. It also brings great gifts like courage and grit whilst its curse is a peculiar kind of loneliness, unable to lower your defences in case someone sees the 'real you'. Never more so than in a corporate culture where 'dogs' will actually eat other 'dogs'.

If that's you, take heart. Your bravado can be turned into the wings of confidence. Remember, chickens can fly!

And, if you don't believe in yourself, how come?

I know it's down to the 'criticisers', even the people who might have said or implied 'I only want what's best for you'. But, that was through their eyes not yours.

I recently learned a great phrase from my book coach, Mindy Gibbins-Klein. She calls people who had, and currently have, a negative and heavy duty impact on you the '*insignificant* others'. I love it! So, use the phrase whenever you feel *as if* someone's putting you down.

And know you can deal with the self-doubt gremlins *and* their allies through your use of language.

> In reality, a word is just a symbol of the energy it carries. Think of the word 'anxious', repeating it a few times in your head. How do you feel?
>
> Clap your hands and shake your body to get rid of that energy.
>
> Now think of the word 'peace', repeating it a few times in your head. How do you feel now?
>
> I guess you won't want to clap hands and shake your body to get rid of this feeling!

So, the language we use ourselves and the language we expose ourselves to is crucially important in how we feel and create our reality. To keep it nourishing and positive...

> Ask yourself if there's an emotional state of being or a personality characteristic which you would like to have right now and don't, what would that be? Take the first thing you get even if you don't understand why that one came.
>
> Could be confidence, acceptance, love, courage, humour... or absolutely anything! You are unique and what you get will be right for you. Except if you get anything negative, like 'sadistic'. Discard it because that's the gremlins playing tricks on you.

If you get two words, see if they work together. Phrases like 'calmly confident' also describe an emotional state.

If they don't work together, choose the one word which is most attractive to you, which draws you back to it again and again. That's the one which will incorporate the other even if it's not immediately obvious how it does.

Now you have your special word write it on loads of post-its. Lower case letters are read more easily and speedily than capitals and I'm all for making things easier and quicker for your brain to process.

Incidentally, choose pastel post-its rather than neon or high colour ones. It's important the word gets priority in processing rather than the colour. And watch out for negative associations with some colours too. Red, for example, has different meanings in different cultures.

Place a post-it where-ever you're most likely to see it.

At home by the kettle, in clothes' drawers, beside light switches, on the mirror in which you shave or make-up or both!

On your person in your wallet, in your purse, in your glasses case, in a notebook and on the dashboard of your car.

Place it on your desk at work. I've told inquisitive colleagues in the past it was my motivational word for the month... which it was. Place your post-its in drawers, in folders you use often and near your computer screen and keyboard.

Anywhere but anywhere where you can see your chosen word, the emotional state of being and the energy you want more of in your life.

Keep it up until you realise your state is now more in line with your word than you could have ever imagined when you began this exercise.

This is an excellent technique to negate the wing clipping gremlins and help reinforce your new and creative shticks.

I spoke about whole brain processing in the Introduction and how you can programme in what you want. With this technique, your eyes read the word consciously to begin with and, when you're used to it, unconsciously.

The word registers inside your brain and your brain responds with, "OK then... you want some 'confidence' or 'peace' or 'enthusiasm'? With pleasure, I'll work on it!" And it does, eventually evoking thoughts and feelings in line with the energy of your word.

And to be a chicken that can fly, avoid the water cooler people like the plague. Most of them congregate around it to whinge and gossip. Remember the power of language? These people are what I call the 'pull you downers' who collude wonderfully with your gremlins, trances and shticks.

They're generally only interested in criticism, negativity and carrying on robotically intheirboxes. Yes, there might be the laughs but at what or at whose expense? So whatever you do, avoid casting your pearls before these swine because they'll only ridicule you and your ideas... generally behind your back.

A wise manager once told me, "If they're talking about someone else in front of you, you can bet they'll be taking about *you* in front of someone else."

Who are the 'pull you downers' with whom you work and how do you feel when you're around them? Not great, I'll bet.

So, when you have to work with them have as little contact as possible. And if one's sitting opposite you or in the office next to you, stick a rich foliaged plant between you and them. It's a great reminder to keep a good strong boundary between your energy and theirs.

If the 'pull you downer' is your boss... you're in trouble! Have minimal contact with him or her and get loads of contact with the kind of people who can counteract their negative energy. They're the kind of people who can help you fly and I call them your delicious 'pull you uppers'.

They're the people who are generally enthusiastic, have a positive attitude towards life and are living it to the best. They're also the people who'll be interested to know you and hear about your ideas. And, when you have friends as 'pull you uppers', they'll give you straight feedback in a creative and constructive way.

Who are the 'pull you uppers' with whom you work and how do you feel when you're around them? YES! Now make a conscious decision to spend more time in their company and, whenever there's a choice, to work more with them.

Remember... the people you mix with are highly influential to what you think, feel and do. Choose the 'uppers'!

As I've mentioned before, another way to hobble yourself and deny your outtayerbox YOU, your purpose, passion and power is through the language you use.

Think of the last time you said, "I can't..." to yourself about something at work. Could be, "I can't head that meeting." Could be, "I can't apply for that post, I'm not good enough." Could be, "I can't talk to Harrison. He doesn't listen to a word I say."

Run your 'I can't' statement through your mind a few times and notice how your body reacts to it and the feelings 'I can't' evoke in you.

Yes, do it now!

I know you don't want to which is precisely why it's a very good idea to do it. Whenever you get an adverse reaction, it's always a good place to go exploring. It's always your cutting edge for growth and developing outtayerbox YOU.

Because 'I can't' always leaves you shut-down and a victim of circumstances... purposeless, passionless and powerless!

Experiment now by saying the same thing to yourself, only, this time, start the sentence with 'I won't'.

Could be, "I won't head that meeting". Could be, "I won't apply for that post even though I am good enough". (Notice how I turned that old shtick around). Could be, "I won't talk to Harrison although he does listen to what I say." (And that one!)

Run your 'I won't' statement through your head a few times and notice how your body reacts to it and any feelings you might have. Different again, isn't it?

'Can't' means you're helpless. 'Won't' means you've got volition and have made a decision not to... that you have choice. And to be outtayerbox YOU and live your purpose you need that volition, that ability to make decisions and have choice.

Because I'm outrageously mischievous, I'm going to encourage you to use your 'I won't' statement to yourself at work. This will flex and develop the muscles of your volition, of your Will, which we'll come to later. Enjoy every moment and, who knows, you might say a few "I won't" statements out loud!

Finally, experiment saying your statement again only, this time, begin it with the words 'I can'. "I can head that meeting." "I can apply for that post." "I can talk to Harrison and have him listen to what I say."

I CAN opens up a universe of total possibilities *and* probabilities to enable you to spread your very magnificent wings and fly.

And, as long as you take care of yourself, balancing energy out with energy in, experiment with saying "I can" at work and notice the difference. If you're not already, you'll find you become one of the 'pull you uppers' who attract others like you to create a supportive 'let's go for it' community. An ideal environment for your personal and professional development.

A client of mine was working in an open office near to a male colleague who was often on the phone. His conversations were basically bitching about everything and anything inside the work place... and outside it. My client had spoken to him several times having been disturbed by his loud conversations and 'could he tone it down a bit please'. Each request was made without success.

When we explored how my client was communicating so as *not* to get heard, he discovered he was a 'farm reared chicken, wings clipped and unassertive'. His lack of self-belief and wishy-washy language guaranteed to let him down. Even his body posture was hobbled, kind of curled into himself. Experiment with that one and see how *you* feel.

He turned the situation around by first getting into a confident emotional state. He simply remembered a time when he had been confident, explored what his confident self was like and then 'stepped' into his confident body posture. Plus, very importantly, he adopted an 'I CAN' attitude before speaking to his colleague about the telephone conversations.

And the coup de grâce? He changed his language, the words and phrases he used from...

'I can't get on with my work when you're on the phone because you speak so loudly. Do you think you could try to turn it down a bit?'

To...

'I imagine you don't realise what a strong and powerful voice you have or the way other people, including me, lose concentration because your conversation grabs our attention. I know you will want to co-operate with me and your other colleagues and that you will remember to lower your voice from now on, won't you?'

Experiment saying the before and after statement out loud. Notice what was different in your experience between the two.

Now go one step further.
Imagine being in my client's situation.
In your mind's eye see yourself confidently and assertively speaking to your colleague in that open office.
Notice how you look, how you sound and how you feel as you confidently deal with the situation.
Notice how your colleague responds positively to you.

Notice how you feel as you walk back to your
desk having achieved what you set out to
accomplish.
Now jot down your experiences in this exercise.
What did you learn?
And what will you do differently in the future
because of that learning?

You might also like to create a few key words to remind
you how you confidently achieved your colleague's
co-operation. Remember, words are symbols for the
energy they carry. Those key words can plug you back
into your very 'chickens can fly' attitude, delivery and
achievement any time you want.

And keep the key words on you at all times as an easy
reminder of how you can connect with your outtayerbox
YOU and stop hobbling.

Lastly, in order to fly at work, to be who you
really are AND enjoy it, don't just be good... BE
OUTSTANDING!

So, how do you do that? Simple!

Some time ago I saw a real tear-jerking story on
YouTube. It was about a young guy with learning
difficulties who got himself a job as a packer in his
local supermarket. Day after day he noticed how the
customers herded into the check-outs while the cashier
worked at speed to get each of them through and out
the other side.

So, he thought about how he could make the paying experience more enjoyable for customers. He checked it out with his Dad who was delighted by his son's initiative and agreed to help him.

The young guy found a load of inspirational quotations which he and his Dad typed into documents on his PC. He then printed them out on different pastel coloured papers and cut them up so each quotation was separate.

The next day at work, every time he packed a customer's bag he would drop one of his quotations into it without saying a thing. He knew they'd find it unpacking their groceries and hoped it would give them a little joy to associate with their check-out experience.

He did it the next day, and the next day, and the one after that. Six days in and something strange began to happen. The store manager noticed that one of her checkouts was getting more customers going through it than others for no apparent reason.

Then, after about two weeks, the store manager noticed that one of her check-outs was getting far more traffic than the others with a long queue forming. Even when she opened an adjacent checkout, most of the queue stayed just where they were.

Plus people in the queue were easy, talking with each other, sharing jokes and having rich conversations. Very unlike their normal 'heads-down-just-let's-get-this-chore-done' normal attitude. And some of them even hugged the young packer after and, sometimes, even before he packed their bag.

Clearly, happier customers were a bonus and the store manager wanted to know how this strange phenomenon was occurring. So, she called a meeting with the cashiers to explore what was going on.

Despite her best questioning 'techniques', nobody could tell her the difference which was making the difference. Well... there was some-one who could. That some-one was a cashier who enjoyed holding out until the very end. (I understand there was some interpersonal and very inyerbox stuff between the two!)

Anyhow, this cashier had spent time talking with the young guy and getting to know him. This cashier had also seen him put something into shopping bags. She'd asked him what he was doing and, when she learned what it was, whole-heartedly supported him. And, whenever possible, she'd make sure the young guy packed bags at her till when she was on duty.

Eventually she said, "Ask the young guy. He knows the secret about why customers he packs bags for are usually happy."

This isn't rocket science. The young guy took his packing seriously. He was, in fact, more than an everyday packer, finding the most efficient and balanced way to pack bags to help 'his' customers in their shopping chore.

He packed the bags because he was thinking way beyond profit. He put his customers' emotional wellbeing at the front and focused on how to turn a mundane task into a pleasing experience.

He took it even a step further and did something outstanding. He gave them, from the deepness of his own being, a gift to warm the deepness of their being. An inspirational surprise to find at home... and to look forward to when next they shopped.

The young guy went way beyond functionality and profit to create and build loving relationship between himself and those he served.

And if you want to be a chicken that can fly, think on. How could you gift your work and the people you serve with something outstanding from yourself, your outtayerbox YOU, which will bring joy to them and a joy to yourself in the giving?

THERE IS ALWAYS SOMETHING!

Along with all the other aspects of this book, it will most definitely reward you a million-fold of what you give. It will reward you through living and serving your purpose at work as only you can live it and serve... for yourself and others.

CHAPTER 14 – IMPASSION YOUR PASSION
WHAT IT'S NOT

'Chase down your passion like it's the last bus of the night.'
Terri Guillemets

So what is passion? And are we on very dodgy territory even talking about it?

Because, historically, passion hasn't had a very good press. The word is often associated by Christians to the suffering of Christ before the last supper and then on the cross. And the word itself originates from the Latin 'patior' meaning to suffer or endure.

That's a million miles away from the other and more steamy meaning for passion. In Victorian England, passion was regarded as something improper in 'respectable' women while highly desirable in women who were not.

It's also nonsense that passion is so often associated with only 'negative' emotions which aren't negative at all, just perceived as such. Anything from anger to lust, from hatred to any 'dark' emotion assumed alien to your nature or usual behaviour.

I bet there's been a time when you've acted in a way that so caught you by surprise you said, 'I don't know what got into me!' Especially if that happened at work where everyone's behaviour comes under the office gossip's scrutiny.

As I mentioned in an earlier chapter, it wasn't something which got into you. It was something which got *out* of you. And, sometimes, that's raw, unadulterated passion.

And passion's just as present in strong love, in enthusiasm, desire, strong commitment or any feeling which enthuses you or inspires you or calls you to action. Without passion you and I are dead. Or at least 'living dead'!

Extreme? I don't think so.

If you've ever been depressed you'll know that it's truly about 'living dead' mentally, emotionally, psychologically and spiritually.

Depression is without colour or richness even to the point of feeling yourself in meaningless wastelands, without purpose or hope; that 'dark night of the soul'. It's about feeling lifeless, numbed, a zombie.

And it doesn't even have to be that extreme. You'll probably know people who live a life of low grade depression year after year after year. You'll recognise them at work as those who do what they have to do in a lacklustre way, going through the motions, without putting any of their self into what they're doing.

While you'll know yet others who aren't depressed but are separated from their feelings. It's like someone cut their throats so they appear to live in their heads.

They're all thought, ideas and mental whirring without the embodied warmth of feelings and emotions such as passion.

If you happen to be a more feeling person, you and they are unlikely to communicate very well unless it's on cut and dried topics. Passion? It just doesn't compute for them.

And that makes me so mad! Now *there's* a good dose of passion and see what language our culture has given passion. 'Mad'! Even I fall into that particular linguistic trap. Because passion is most definitely not about being or going mad.

In this case, for 'mad', read being full of passionate and righteous anger. For nobody but nobody taught me, or you, as a child how to access, harness and creatively channel our passionate energy, our birthright and our heritage. It's your essential life energy which you need to be able to turn your purpose into real things and actions in the world.

Unless you were really lucky, you would have learned quite the opposite. In varying degrees, in one way or another, you were most likely taught to sit on your passion, to squash it as something not quite acceptable or OK.

Some of you, like me, were even taught to murder your passion for the sake of being well-behaved, quiet, not asking questions, not choosing the incorrect education path or wrong job/career trajectory... blah-blah-blah-blah-blah!

The good news is there is absolutely no way you could have *really* killed off your passion. Although you probably hid it so very well to protect its integrity that often you've forgotten where you put it in the first place.

The even more good news is, once you know your purpose, it acts like a pair of bellows breathing life into the seemingly dying embers of your hidden passion.

So it's crucial you remind yourself your passion is always just a hair's breadth away. It's always but always that close to your reach!

> Remember a time when you were feeling healthily passionate.
>
> Could be as a child running down a sunny beach into the sea.
> Could be hearing some music which stirred you up emotionally and filled your heart to bursting.
> Could be seeing someone you love and feeling the depth of your affection and desire to care for them.
> Could be scoring that great goal or completing that important project.
>
> Remember and re-experience your passionate event.

There it is!

There's your passion right in front of your nose, alive, vibrant and contained in a memory. For when you remember with your passion then it's here... *right now.* Always, always, your passion is just a hair's breadth away.

Remember too that passion can be as soft as a gentle breeze through your hair as well as the vigour of wind whizzing through it in an open top sports car. Even if dictionaries generally define its meaning as a 'powerful or compelling emotion'. What do they know?

> Remember a time when your passion was a bit like melting cheese, still as substantial but way softer than scoring a goal.
>
> Could be a feeling you had when reflecting on some poignant or compassionate time in your life.
> Could be learning of an injustice at work which left you more sorrowful than angry.
> Could be seeing or hearing about some natural disaster with people for whom you can feel for as a fellow human being.
>
> Remember and experience.

That's your passion too!

What passion most definitely isn't is all the negative associations and negative dictionary definitions which have been applied to it. They refer to how you can use your passion for the bad rather than the good and have nothing at all to do with what your passion actually is.

CHAPTER 15 – IMPASSION YOUR PASSION
SO, WHAT IS IT THEN?

*'There is no passion to be found playing small –
In settling for a life that is less than the one you are
capable of living.'*

Nelson Mandela

Passion is your essential life energy. It's the difference between whether you feel alive in the world or dead. So it's closely allied with being outtayerbox YOU. Indeed, passion is the very breath of outtayerbox YOU.

I want to hang my head outside my office window and yell all the way to yours, "You will feel unbelievably more alive and vital when you connect to and live your passion."

And, when you know your purpose, you cannot *not* be passionate!

Purpose gives you a cause and meaning for your life and attracts your passion like a bee to sweet pollen.

My definition of passion has it squarely as the animating or vital principle in human beings. The word comes from the Latin 'spiritus' meaning soul, courage, vigour, breath. And this has absolutely nothing to do with religion as in organised religions unless, of course, you want it to be related to your religion. In which case, you'll find lots of connections.

The passion I'm talking about transcends and is way more than the teaching of passion within religion as I've heard it. It is, indeed, your very breath. And when you're connected to your passion it is as if you have life breathed into you when before you were just an automated robot going through the motions.

It never ceases to surprise me how many pale-faced clients I see over the course of a year. That has nothing to do with not having been out in the sun or not eating the right foods. Nor does it have anything to do with skin colour pigmentation as people of all skin colours can look paler than normal. Instead, it's totally to do with a huge lack of purpose, passion and power.

One financial director stands out in my memory. He was in his late 30s, bright and political, having carved out an excellent career path for himself and followed it to the letter. He was also successfully married with two young children. In fact, he was a very ordinary, run of the mill, conforming, 'good boy' doing all that was expected of him.

And he looked like a skeleton. He was under-weight, pale to the point of translucent with lack-lustre eyes that bobbed out of his head for lack of cushioned flesh to sit in.

A real sight! A real parody of what I've been talking about as living dead.

He'd come to me for anxiety at work and in his personal life. Whatever he did, whatever he achieved, whatever he experienced, he had a constant underlying anxiety which made no sense to him at all. And perfect sense to me.

He was as dry as a bone, no vital juices and no vigour. No breath to talk of except a shallow excuse for it, gasping in his throat. This is the kind of breathing which goes by the name of breathing when you're stressed or anxious.

It was clear to me that, somehow or another, he'd missed out on connecting with his life energy, his very passion.

I'd be lying if I said he got joined up with his passion as a one session miracle. This degree of living dead is extreme and it takes time to 'warm up'. Because that's exactly what happens when you connect with your passion. You start warming up.

So it was for him. Through reconnecting bit by bit with the vitality and heat of his passion. Over a period of six appointments, I saw him beginning to put on weight and fill out.

By the fourth session, I had him looking straight into the large mirror in my office to notice that his skin now had some tone and texture. He saw there was pinkness in it from blood filling surface capillaries and that his eyes were no longer lacklustre and without cushioning. He was coming alive.

Look around you in the office, even at women who wear make-up. How many pale, low energy faces can you see? And what about yours?

One of the simplest and easiest ways to connect with your passion is through your body...

Run up and down a flight of stairs three times.
Dance to energetic music.
Take a cold shower ... honestly!
Act 'as if' you're a passionate person, copying
body movements, gestures and facial expressions
of some-one who is.

If you're really sharp, you'll have noticed my client
didn't find his purpose before he re-connected with
his passion. I know! I started this book with 'purpose'
because it's so central to having a sense of meaning and
direction to your life.

And, I confess, you can reconnect with your passion
without first knowing your purpose. It's a chicken
before egg or egg before chicken situation.

And... knowing your purpose is literally like putting
that electric plug into the socket and switching on.
Passion lift off is guaranteed.

Because there's one more element of your passion I've
not yet mentioned and that's **enthusiasm**, originating
from the Greek word meaning 'having the god within.'

Yes, it sounds like we're back to organised religion
again and we're not...or we are, depending on your
beliefs. 'God' can mean anything you want it to mean.
Could be a traditional god from your religious beliefs,
a higher power or energy, the essence of nature or the
'ooomph' in the Universe, as I like to call it.

And, when you have enthusiasm for something,
you're inspired to take action about whatever it is which

inspires you. You're inspired to turn your vision into reality.

'Inspired' itself comes from the Latin 'inspirare', to breathe... here's that taking breath thing again. Ancient meanings include to 'breathe on' and 'breathe life into'. Meanings which fit perfectly with what your passion does for you.

Remember a time when you were feeling passionate with enthusiasm. In your mind's eye, see yourself being gorgeously passionate with enthusiasm at that time.

Take a few moments to explore how you look, how you feel and how you sound being enthusiastically passionate

When you're ready, let the image of yourself fade and, as it does, let outtayerbox YOU give you a symbol for your enthusiastic passion. Take whatever comes, however bizarre or nonsensical it might seem... and explore the features of your symbol whatever it is.

Lastly, your passion has a very positive message for you. A message which might come as words, movement, pictures, colours, sounds... anything at all in your imagination. Take whatever it is, knowing you will logically understand the message later if you don't understand it immediately.

Let your passion give you its very positive message now.

Describe in words or draw your symbol. Use it in the future to reconnect with your enthusiastic passion whenever you want.

What was your passion's positive message for you?

And in what ways can you have more of your enthusiastic passion at work?

For passion, laced by enthusiasm, is molten gold. It's life energy, soul, courage, vigour, breath, having the god within. The fire in your belly which inspires, influences, motivates and mobilises you, not only to come alive, but to make your mark in the world, however big or however small.

Its size doesn't matter. Making your mark does!

And in case you didn't get it, this is your **soul energy**. Passion is your internal dynamo which came with you when you got physically born and will leave when you physically die. This is about your meaning and purpose... what on earth you're all about!

CHAPTER 16 – IMPASSION YOUR PASSION
HAVING THE HOTS CAN BE GREAT!

'Be still when you have nothing to say; when genuine passion moves you, say what you've got to say, and say it hot.'
David Herbert Lawrence

Yeah, yeah! You normally understand the phrase 'having the hots' as being sexually aroused, fancying some-one like crazy. Correct! So how about having the hots for your purpose and outtayerbox YOU?

And as for being 'aroused', tell me the difference in physiological sensations between...

Footballers jumping all over each other passionately when a goal's been scored, losing yourself dancing to some great music which really gets you moving, having such a great workout at the gym that you are rocking, and...

having the hots for someone!

Aroused or not? Adrenalin and endorphin levels raised or not? Your making-meaning-of-the-world mind will ascribe different meanings to those experiences because of the different contexts. And when it comes down to physiology and emotional experience there's very little difference between them. Well, give a sensation or two!

Which means you can, indeed, have the hots for yourself.

And, if several of your gremlins, trances and shticks are screaming that it's not OK to have the hots for yourself, you've got a choice. You can either agree with them and squash your life energy down again or you can thank them for their interest. Follow up your 'thanks' swiftly by saying, '... and, *right now*, I'm exploring how having the hots for myself is *very* OK!'

Way back, when I started out on my corporate career, I met a fantastic woman. She was vibrant, confident and a very effective manager when women as managers weren't that common at all.

And I remember, particularly, how she had a certain kind of presence, an authority which didn't need her to be loudly vocal or insistent about things. When she said a task had to be done, it got done. When she asked for data to be given to her by a certain date, it arrived on time.

With hindsight, I can see she had great rapport skills, used language effectively and was always clear with her staff about how they were doing and what she expected from them. So everybody knew where they stood with her and she knew where she stood with them.

And, I guess, I saw her as a role model and took every opportunity I could to learn from her. She, in turn, acted as my mentor, generously giving me the benefit of her experience and knowledge.

It was she who told me the #1 golden rule of being an effective manager. The #1 rule is having the hots for yourself and your work which can, in turn, inspire and motivate your staff to 'have the hots' for the work too.

Because having passion and enthusiasm for your work turns any task into an adventure, a possibility for learning and enjoyment. Even more, having the hots for yourself, being aroused by your outtayerbox YOU and your purpose, turns your job into a vehicle to make your mark on the world, however big or however small.

I remember being a bit shocked and saying something like, "Isn't it selfish to have the hots for yourself?" as if focusing on yourself was a cardinal sin. Which, of course, it's certainly deemed to be in certain quarters. Having the hots for yourself even gets called egocentric or narcissistic which are, in fact, psychological pathologies.

She laughed deliciously. "Of course it's very selfish! And by that I mean 'self-ish', taking care of yourself so you can be the most of yourself you can be and living life to the full."

And being alive, as fully YOU as you can be, is certainly passion central!

In reality, I suspect that people who are pathologically egocentric or narcissistic are a very long way from having the hots about their outtayerbox YOU or their purpose. Their affliction is about me, me, me and, for narcissism, am I not the best, most gorgeous, most superb of creatures?

These conditions are not about living your purpose for yourself and others or feeling so fully alive you could jump with joy.

And I don't say 'jump for joy' for no good reason. For there are two further good things I want to mention about having the hots for yourself.

The first good thing is you can experience 'it', your passion and enthusiasm, through your body and feelings, as I mentioned in the last chapter... *and* through your mind.

> Think of a time when you were fully engaged and using your body for dancing, for sport or for some other physical activity where you built up a steam. What were your body sensations like and how did you feel?
>
> Think of a time when you were inspired and passionate about something or someone. Could be 'falling in love' with a leisure activity, a hobby, or a person. What were your feelings like at that time?
>
> Now think of a time when you were engaged on an intellectual project of some kind.
>
> Could be something which required your intellect at work. Could be writing an essay, a thesis, a story, or even a report. Could be following instructions to create something.

Now remember how it felt when you knew you'd cracked it... you'd got it! What was the 'feeling' experience like in your mind?

If at least one of the above wasn't 'orgasmic' in some way, I'd encourage you to let go a little. Having the hots can truly impassion your life and help develop your potential... if you let it!

A friend who had visited Cuba told me how every night people would go out on the streets making music and dancing their socks off. People of all ages, all shapes and all sizes. She described many of them as amazing dancers who got lost in their dancing dancing dancing. Bodies moving rhythmically and abandoningly.

That made absolute sense to me. They lived in a heritage of poverty and deprivation, often in crumbling-decaying-splendour or shanty towns, earning little and with food rationing. And dancing is an escape from humdrum reality, a gateway into glory, a gateway into your passion, a gateway into feeling so alive, so sexy.

And what about your passionate feelings?

Most usually you associate passionate feelings with another person, with being 'in love' or lusting after them. And, as you'll have experienced through the exercises, there are many more ways to experience passion in our feelings than that.

Some people have passionate feelings during religious worship. You might have experienced passionate feelings following your favourite sports person or football team. Still others have passionate feelings listening to certain music, seeing particular works of art or experiencing fast driving.

I once worked with a man who was passionate about social justice and worked stoically in the field of politics to help there be more of it in the world. He told me that his feelings were like standing under a giant waterfall, totally in awe of its beauty. And every time he experienced his passion it motivated him to find innovative ways to bring even more social justice into the world.

People usually understand how you could get your rocks off with passion in your body or your feelings... but in your mind!? Hopefully you had a taste of that in the last exercise. And there's more.

Years ago I had a colleague who was married to a mathematician. This was not your everyday kind of maths. He worked with the concepts behind everyday maths, delving into vast swirling hinterlands of conceptual mathematics like the mysteries of the black hole. And he said maths was as sexy as hell!

I think Einstein would have agreed with him. Because he was one of many innovators who reported the passion of research and discovery. And I'm sure you will also know of Eureka moments in your own life when you really 'got' something.

I remember writing my Masters Degree dissertation which was research into the use of humour in psychotherapy. Yes, despite the popular image of therapy, the use of humour, applied appropriately and ethically, is highly effective.

And I remember getting my rocks off intellectually as bits of theory became clear and fitted together with my research findings and what they meant. I can even reconnect with that 'Wahooooooo!' feeling in my memory as I write about it now. Mind passion can be so invigorating.

The second good thing about having the hots for yourself is other people will then also have them for you... in the best possible way. I don't mean that the hordes will descend to rip off your clothes and ravage you... unless of course you want to encourage that.

What I do mean is that, if you live in your passion, you cannot help but inspire and motivate other people to come fully alive and live in their passion too. You become like a flame which attracts moths that see the light in you, recognise its energy and, very understandably, desire some of it for themselves.

As my American sister would say, "Goooood job!"

Because, whatever your purpose is, it is most definitely for the benefit of yourself AND others.

And whatever your purpose is, it's the vehicle through which you can come fully alive and express your passion. Whatever it is, you're role modelling that positive and very healthy shtick for anyone with eyes to see and ears to hear. Just like that woman manager did for me so long ago.

Now isn't *that* worth having the hots for yourself for?

Your passion, in an even bigger sense, is about your even bigger mission in life to be the most you can be.

Am I mad? Yes, remember that I am most definitely mad about you being the most you can be because you are not an insignificant human being, one among millions.

You are most uniquely outtayerbox YOU with a particular purpose and passion to achieve in the world and your work.

> Three stone-cutters were building a house of worship in the middle ages. The project's architect noticed the three men's work differed from good to excellent. And their individual batches of cut stone also seemed to carry differing energies.

> Being a curious man, he decided to explore what was behind the differences in the quality of their cutting energy. So he spoke to the first stone-cutter who did good work although it had an everyday quality to it. The kind of work any other good stone-cutter would do.

> The architect asked him, "What are you doing when you're cutting stone for this project?" And the first stone-cutter said, "I'm just cutting the stone."

> The architect understood this was the reason this man's work was so every day, without panache or pizzazz. He was just cutting stone.

> The second stone cutter's work was above every day. It was very good and there was a certain warmth and passion about its energy.

When asked, the second stone-cutter replied, "I am earning money to support and feed my wife and children."

And the architect understood that, with this aim in mind, the man's love for his family got cut into the stones as well.

Then the architect approached the third stone-cutter whose work had impressed him by its excellence and extra something, something he couldn't quite put a finger on.

When asked the question, the third stone-cutter stopped for a moment. He picked up a piece of stone which lay at his feet as if it were the most precious thing in the entire world.

And, looking straight into the eyes of the architect, back straight and head held high, he said, "I am building a cathedral."

The architect immediately understood that with this bigger mission, with the third stone-cutter experiencing himself as part of a majestic endeavour, his purpose and his passion were also cut into every piece of stone he carved.

That was the difference which made the difference. The excellent stone cutter had the hots for his purpose, his passion *and* himself.

Which stone-cutter are you? And which stone-cutter do you want to be?

Above all else... have the hots for *your* purpose, *your* passion and *your*self.

Have the hots for outtayerbox YOU!

CHAPTER 17 – POWER
OUT OF KILTER

'When sitting, sit. When walking, walk.
Whatever you do, don't wobble.'

Zen saying

There's an old saying to understand what something is you first have to understand what it is not. And perhaps nothing could be truer when it comes to the thorny issue of power.

You're out of kilter, not functioning fully, and inyerbox you when you're not being powerful. You're out of kilter when you're not behaving or experiencing yourself as causal in the world but at the mercy of it and other people. And, at such times, you'll find yourself pointing the finger at work.

You can't do this because x hasn't done y. One of your direct reports is 'unmanageable' and that's got nothing to do with you. You can't go ahead with this project because...

Because, because, because! Excuses and rationalisations to explain away why you're not taking your personal power and influencing what goes on around here.

Powerful! Who me?

Regrettably, 'power' got a bad name around you... and me.

First, there's the cultural hangover from the Victorian era, colonialism and the authoritarian attitudes of political, business and industrial leaders which influenced worldwide. Add to that our awareness of tyrants and despots, past and present, who have influenced our perceptions on power.

And then there's 'parenting', whether by blood or association. I don't see how anyone in our culture who's been a child could have avoided being bullied. Because that's what parents do.

They make you do things you don't want to do like going to bed when you're wide awake. They make you behave in ways which you don't want to behave, like tomboys being forced to wear girly stuff and more sensitive boys being made to toughen up. And for some children there's much worse, including severe mental, emotional, physical and sexual abuse.

What you learned about power was it hurt or distressed you. It was about coercion, dominance, control and fear making.

And that wasn't power. It was a gross distortion of power.

So, you grew up as someone who didn't like confrontation, who was more likely to buckle against that kind of behaviour. Or you grew up as someone who became a bully, repeating what was done to you to others. Or you grew up as someone who resolved to learn how to use your power creatively and wisely... and did.

Don't tell me you don't have the capacity to be a bully! Everyone who's been bullied, everyone who at some time has been a victim of bullying, has internalised the ability to be a bully.

A manager in the public sector was referred to me for having 'difficulty in relationships'. What a euphemism. She was in her thirties, ambitious, good looking, well presented and a definite go-getter.

Up until now, relationships at work had not seemed a problem... to her. And in this, her first pretty important managerial role, she couldn't understand why there had been mutterings about her and a rising number of sick absences in her team.

When I explored with her the challenges she was having and how she might be behaving at work, the situation became pretty clear.

Firstly, nobody had taught her how to manage effectively which is a common oversight in organisations. Her promotion had been based on merit, on the great work she'd been doing in another department with the assumption she could, of course, 'manage'.

Secondly, she'd based her managerial style on the one with which she was most familiar. She'd modelled her previous authoritarian boss and her historically authoritarian father.

Despite the distress both had caused her at times, the strong impact of these models over all others resulted in her unconsciously identifying with them. She was primed ready to regurgitate bullying behaviour as and when she deemed it necessary.

Recognising what she was doing was a big whack around the head and the first step towards her recovery. Happily, her 'waking up' also enabled her to connect with her own and very healthy, natural powerfulness.

True power empowers other people. It doesn't make them victims.

What amazes me is bullies seem generally tolerated by management at work. It's usually the victims of work place bullying who are referred for therapy or coaching when sorting the bullies would be far more cost effective.

Correction! It's not amazing.

Remember... parenting in this culture involves bullying so, at some level, everyone in the corporate or organisational structure will have a fear of 'the bully' tucked away somewhere. And, when we fear the bully we're less likely to confront him or her.

And less likely to see the bully in ourselves.

Have you never coerced someone to do something through threat or passively through emotional blackmail along the lines of 'If you don't do this I won't do that?' This is a very common ploy in office politics called 'you scratch my back and I'll scratch yours'.

Although it's usual for the reciprocal back scratch not to happen. Bullies often renege on promises.

Have you never leaned on anyone to achieve what you wanted rather than what would be good for them? And please, please do not think this is just overt behaviour. It can be very subtle, especially for people in positions of power. A look of the eye or a raised eyebrow or a certain comment can be enough.

None of this is about being powerful. It's a distortion of power. It's often what goes by the name of power. AND IT'S NOT POWER!

And, because of all the distortions, you learned to have fear about being powerful yourself, even if you think you are a powerful person. I know that sounds crazy... but, remember, I am crazy for you to be outtayerbox YOU, full of purpose, passion and your *natural* powerfulness. I am crazy about you coming back into kilter.

If you were truly powerful, what then?

Head up a piece of A4 paper with...

If I'm truly powerful...

Say it to yourself at the beginning of every line beneath the heading and then finish the sentence with whatever comes into your mind.

Let yourself be surprised by some of the gremlins, trances and shticks you discover you have about being powerful. They developed BECAUSE OF WHAT YOU LEARNED WHICH WENT BY THE NAME OF POWERFUL BUT WAS NOT POWERFUL!

Do this exercise very quickly to allow whole brain processing access information your inyerbox you won't find palatable. The slower you do it the more likely gremlins, trances and shticks will obstruct your way.

IT'S IMPORTANT!

You need to know what until now has got in the way of you being your natural powerfulness. Then you can do something about those obstructions... or not. It's your choice.

At the times you think you've written as much as you can, keep going. These are precisely the times when you're coming across ingrained gremlins, trances and shticks. Keep repeating to yourself, "If I'm truly powerful...." and see what comes.

When you've got to the point where you feel 'cooked', where there's no emotional charge about going on or stopping... pause.

Read through your list and see what other information comes to your mind about being powerful or powerless. Make notes to remind yourself for the future if need be.

What have you learned?

What do you want to do about what you've learned?

And how will you behave differently in the future
because of that learning?

Now you've 'outted' some of that inhibiting stuff and
worked out how to behave differently, you're ready to
move on. If your old stuff pops into your mind again,
simply thank it for its information and tell it that, *right
now*, you're connecting with your very natural and
elegant powerfulness.

Because, to be *in* kilter, you need to stand in the
ground of your natural power which is associated with
outtayerbox YOU, your purpose and your passion. And
your natural power is nothing like any power you've
come across before. Be prepared to be surprised and
delighted by what you discover.

> Firstly, stand up and vigorously move your arms,
> hands, legs and feet as if you're shaking off a
> pile of unwanted mud after a game of rugby. This
> will make sure none of the gremlins, trances or
> shticks from the last exercise are craftily sticking
> to you.
>
> Keep going with the shaking off until you get the
> 'It's done' signal from outtayerbox YOU.
>
> Now, sit comfortably, spine straight and feet
> squarely on the floor.
>
> Take a few deep breaths and gently relax your
> body... then your feelings... then your mind until
> you find the stillest quietest place inside yourself.

It doesn't have to be totally still or quiet. Just the stillest and quietest place for now.

Then trusting your outtayerbox YOU, take a few more deep breaths in and out. As you do, be aware that your natural power is strong, skilful and good. It's only interest is promoting your wellbeing, your purpose and your passion and taking beneficial action at work and in the world.

Close your eyes and let your imagination give you a very positive symbol for your natural power.

As usual, take whatever you get, however bizarre it might seem. Could be a person, an animal, a 'thing', anything within our universe or outside of it!

Once you get your symbol, take a few moments to explore it, getting to know it and all its features as well as you can. Then open your eyes and record your power symbol in some way... drawing, writing or anything which works for you.

Finally, write down the first three key words which describe your natural power for you.

If you seem to have got nothing, be prepared for insights and realisations about your natural power in the hours and days ahead. Keep your notebook on you at all times!

It's not unusual for people to feel disappointed when they first see or sense their symbol if it's small or not very strong looking. If that was you, jump up and down ten times and change your emotional state for a more energetic one.

It's likely your natural power wasn't given much, if any, air space as you grew up. So, it needs some sun, water and organic fertiliser... all of which you can provide metaphorically. Just imagine giving your symbol whatever it says it needs for its healthy growth.

Because the good news is you can develop your natural power however young or old you are. The even better news is you have now re-connected with your natural power. So, even if you consciously got nothing, the re-connection has taken place and your power is already developing, even as you read these words.

Together with your purpose and your passion, your power will be a creative force in getting the results you want at work and in your life. More of that later.

You've begun to make the connection with your natural power and started exploring what it is. And now, to be able to use it most beneficially, you first need to know how exactly you're giving your power away at work. Oh yes, you are!

CHAPTER 18 - POWER
WAITING FOR WWW.GOD.COM

"Let's go."
"Yes, let's go."
Stage direction: They do not move.

From Waiting For Godot by Samuel Becket

How familiar is that?

How familiar is it for you *not* to take the initiative at work, however small the issue? How familiar is it for you to do the 'it's more than my job's worth' whether subtly or in its grossest form? How familiar is it for you to wait to be told what to do?

How familiar is it for you to say that you would take the initiative if only you weren't blocked, stymied or generally trapped by your circumstances?

That's what I call giving your power away!

I remember in my early days working with managers who were trained specifically to 'act on command'. The management structure was hierarchical, protective and stifling of initiative. The command chain went up and up and up and up. And this can happen, even now, in all sorts of organisations, corporate, public, third sector... any sector.

I wasn't happy in that assignment and, in retrospect, would have been better off not to have taken the contract. But I was young and eager, and thought, even if organisational values weren't aligned with mine, I could do some good. And I could... but in whose eyes???

I remember so distinctly one manager who stood apart from the rest in having been conditioned to be a 'good boy' and had only done what he was told to do from his cradle to this post. So much so, he couldn't respond to even the most minor event without referring to his own manager... just to check he was doing 'it' right.

Needless to say, this had become an organisational problem. His was an extreme but not unusual example of personal disempowerment.

In the biggest sense, I call the whole giving-your-power-away-thing the 'waiting for www.god.com' syndrome.

Out there in cyberspace somewhere, an imagined source of direction, the biggest website operation ever conceived. You might be working on some thorny issue. And, just like that manager, you might be hoping on hope for some authority to turn up and show you how to crack it, to get it 'right'.

Because, just like the actors in Beckett's play, you could be waiting for A.N.Other. In this case an A.N.Other who'll be effective and influential and who will take responsibility for you and your life. Just like in the play, that person is an A.N.Other who never arrives. And, if you get stuck in that wishful thinking, you will certainly remain powerless and inert.

I can understand that. You've already explored some of the gremlins, trances and shticks associated with you being powerful. They all have a part to play for your particular version of 'waiting for www.god.com'.

If you're more female, it might be the old myth of the knight on the white charger who's going to rescue you from having to deal with all the challenging stuff which goes on in your life. If you're more male, it might be a variation on the theme of being recognised by a major football talent scout who whisks you away to seemingly effortless fame and fortune.

I'm not saying that never happens... but in what universe? And what price do you have to pay, to whose gremlins, trances and shticks do you have to conform for the bondage of powerlessness?

And now I enter www.god.com on my internet and, what do you know, there is such a site. You'd think it would be all Michelangelo, richness of colour and image, inspiring and motivational. In reality it's anything but. A dreary, rather stilted and unappealing site.

And, maybe, that's part of the problem. Rather than take your power at work, you're waiting for a fanfare, an 1812 overture blast of fireworks and hosannas that will herald your purpose... and then do the rest for you.

It's quite simple. There you are waiting for www.god.com to inform you of what precisely you have to do to fulfil your purpose. And, if you haven't uncovered that one yet, you're even hoping for the full Monty of a job spec which also tells you what on earth you're here for.

That's not going to happen!

The only person who *will* make it happen is you. And the way you will make it happen is through connecting with outtayerbox YOU, your purpose, your passion AND your power.

Do I hear your gremlins, trances and shticks slink away with their tails between their legs like a pantomime character evoking sympathy? Yeah, yeah, yeah!

Once there was a man caught up in an enormous flood. So devastating was it, the only safe place to be was sitting on the roof of his house. He was hungry and cold though he'd wrapped himself in dustbin liners as some measure of protection against the wind and rain which continued to bucket down.

After a while, he saw something floating towards him in the water. He squinted as hard as he could as he was sure it looked like a person. And, as the thing got nearer, he recognised a woman holding onto a huge tree trunk, straddling it like a cowboy riding her horse.

As she got near she shouted out to the man, "The water's taking me right past your roof. Jump on my log. It's got plenty of room for two and the water's flow is moving towards town where I'm sure we'll get help."

The man waved and shouted back to her,
"Thanks so much for your kind offer but I
know my god will save me." And they both
wished each other well on their way.

Sometime later, he was feeling a little lonely.
His stomach was beginning to rumble for lack
of food when he noticed something else on the
water which was moving purposefully towards
him.

As it got closer, he recognised a small family
in a four oared boat moving lithely forward.
The father and mother called out to him to
join them as there was certainly room for one
more.

But, waving them on, and thanking them for
their kindness, the man called out back to
them, "Go well on your way as I know my
god will save me." So they rowed purposefully
past him on his roof, the children waving
good-naturedly as they disappeared into the
distance.

After a while it began to get darker, the kind of
early afternoon winter darkness which heralds
an early nightfall in the northern hemisphere.
And the man admitted to himself he was
getting afraid. The water had crept over the
guttering of his roof and he'd had to move up
higher to avoid getting wet.

Suddenly, he heard the whirr of something in the distance which was lighting up the sky and he just knew it had to be a helicopter. Indeed, it was and, picking him up in their search light, the crew made a beeline for him.

The helicopter hovered over his roof as one of the crew came down on a cable to take him to safety. The crew member was astonished when the man refused help.

"Are you insane?" he gasped. "The rain's still falling, the water level will rise and there's not much more roof to go. Let us take you with us."

But the man was absolutely adamant in refusing the crew member's attempts to get him into the safety harness. "No!" said the man firmly. "My god will save me!"

Eventually and very reluctantly the crew member gave up. He concluded the man was, indeed, insane and without the aid of a doctor to sedate him there was no way they could help him to safety. So, his colleagues wound him back up into the belly of the helicopter which then left to search for people more willing to be rescued.

The rain continued until, inch by inch, the water covered the man's roof and there was nowhere else for him to go but into the icy water where, very shortly, he drowned.

On arriving at the pearly gates, he demanded of St Peter he be taken to god immediately. St Peter had been forewarned of his arrival and swiftly heralded him into the inner chamber. God smiled at him benevolently and asked him what he needed.

"Need!" cried out the man, "Need! I believed in you. I believed you would come and rescue me but you didn't!"

God went very quiet for a moment and then, with a firm and patient voice, replied, "I sent you a log. Then I sent you a boat. And *then* I sent you a helicopter. What else did you want of me???"

Perhaps the man on the roof was another person waiting for the 1812 Overture and a mega fireworks' display to herald the miraculous happening of their rescue. I sort of understand refusing a log. I can even understand refusing a boat, if it looked perilous. But a helicopter!?

I think it was Woody Allen who said, "80% of success is just turning up." You have to take the opportunities as they present themselves. Turn up! Grab your power by its balls and just TURN UP!

Turning up is not about being in body only with the rest of you AWOL. That's about *having* to do or be something, about duty, about responsibility (the heavy kind which wears on your ears) or a 'must' because it's expected of you.

And being only in body reminds me of registration at school when the form teacher would very tiredly call out everyone's name, one by one, and you would reply something like, "Present, Miss." Yawn yawn. Repetition boredom.

Truly turning up is the absolute opposite of 'waiting for www.god.com'.

When you turn up as outtayerbox YOU standing in your power, it's all about you being very present and engaged in who you are and what you're doing. Truly turning up gives you a state of curiosity and openness. Who knows what adventure might evolve from you just being YOU and being there... where ever 'there' is?

And, for sure, when you truly turn up as outtayerbox YOU, standing robustly in your power, you most definitely won't miss opportunities... unless they're the kind of opportunities you choose to miss!

> What stops you turning up in your power at work?

> What can you do to triumph over or get round those obstructions?

> What do you need to help you do that?

> When do you turn up at work standing in your power?

> In what situations?

With whom?

And how can you get more of that at work?

GO GET IT!

Having done this exercise, what have you learned about outtayerbox YOU and turning up at work in your power? And what will you do differently in the future?

Because you will, won't you?

Because turning up in your power is so very sexy.

And here's how...

CHAPTER 19 – POWER
TO WILL OR NOT TO WILL!

A man can do all things if he but wills them.

Leon Battista Alberti

.

How often have you heard the phrase 'where there's a will there's a way'? And there always is. Yet having will is not always welcomed by parents or society at large, although males traditionally seem to get away with it more than females in my culture.

Boys can exert their will and be thought of as a 'lad'. Girls, on the other hand, are often told they're aggressive when, in fact, they're just being assertive.

And, irrespective of gender, some families just don't like children making choices and their own decisions. If this was your family, it's likely you were told you were too 'wilful', too sure of yourself, too cocky, too big for your boots.

If that's been the case, it's time for you to change and energise your power.

This Will is 'will' with a capital W. It's not just any old will as in 'you will do this!' or 'his will is broken'. That 'will' carries a message of force, lack of choice and bending your will to somebody else's... or else! It means living somebody else's wants, needs and life instead of your own.

You might have come across this kind of will in some working environments where there's autocratic management. If you have, you'll also have come across stress, fear, lack of motivation and enjoyment at work. Plus, usually high sick absence figures.

With a bit of luck, you'll also have come across a subversive sub-culture which sabotages that management's initiatives. Not great for productivity but an excellent example of a self-starting morale booster and a distorted form of Will through sticking two fingers up at management. Corporate teenage rebellion!

However, the Will I'm talking about is the power of *choosing* your own actions. It's involved in purpose and determination, in the Will to succeed. This Will is the ability to observe what's going on without bias. And then determine, or choose, to act in line with what's appropriate for the situation and right for you.

You might often reply to a request to do something with a straight yes or no. Sometimes that's appropriate when the thing in hand needs dealing with swiftly or the choice is so apparent it's a no-brainer.

And, there's a third choice beyond yes or no, a third response to requests for your time, energy and effort, which you might not use nearly often enough. It goes something like, "I'll think about that and come back to you."

This gives you the time and space to do precisely what you said. You take some time to think about what's the right choice, the right thing to do for you *and* the right course of action *for you* in that particular situation.

I've worked with many people in organisations who complain that they're snowed-under, over-worked and stressed. No sooner do they think they've got on top of stuff than their boss gives them another pile. Or they're allocated another area to oversee. Or they're given another project to manage. Sound familiar?

There's a magic question which gets many of my clients every time... "Do you ever say no?" They usually answer either 'rarely' or 'never'. An answer which means they, and perhaps you, rarely if ever use your Will.

Without realising you have a Will, or using it, you're you inyerbox. You'll feel impotent, even a 'victim', with other people and other things having control over you.

Your one wish is to avoid as much struggle, pain and effort as possible. But, paradoxically, by having this very short term wish, you create even more struggle, pain and effort for yourself. Just like those people who complain they're snowed-under, overworked and stressed because they never say no!

Incidentally, the way forward is to make a list of everything for which you're responsible, directing or doing personally. The next time your manager gives you something on top of that, show them your list.

Then ask them, given you're working at maximum and you'd hate them to contravene 'duty of care', which of the things on your list do they want you to stop doing so you can do the new thing they've just given you. Watch that space!

Once you understand you have a Will and can make choices, a subtle change happens in your awareness even if you continue not to use your Will. You begin to recognise how you *could* turn up... which is the very beginning of developing personal power.

And it's certainly time, whatever you're doing, whatever job you're in, to begin developing your Will. You do that in exactly the same way you develop your muscles through working out at a gym. Start exercising it...

I once worked professionally with a woman who was a forceful presence at work to say the least. Not quite Meryl Streep in *The Devil Wears Prada*, but not far off.

And, when it was the right time for me to challenge her use of will... the brute force, manipulative, fear inducing distortion of Will energy... she pooh-poohed me. She didn't hesitate to inform me she didn't need any lessons in the use of Will!

Then one day, through some of my challenges in a particular session, she woke up, looked in the mirror and saw what a bully she was. She recognised what she had previously thought of as willpower was a very dark coercive energy learned from her tyrant of a mother.

She realised she'd taken on board the only way to get ahead and be top dog was to act in a brutal way. Gremlins, trances and shticks again!

The problem was she had done exceedingly well with this approach in her male dominated profession. She was known as the 'Rottweiler'. She was proud of her nickname and to be one of the 'boys'. Yet, at what price?

Those great whacks around the head led her to going back to basics, to learning about her Will and using it ethically and responsibly.

And, to her astonishment, she achieved even greater success acting respectfully in relationship with people rather than being coercive. She went on to greater success through being even more powerful than she ever thought she could have been before.

She did that through developing and using three different aspects of Will in an integrated way. Those three aspects are Strong, Skilful and Good Will

Strong Will is just that. The ability for you to consider, make choices and take action. And sometimes you will do things which you don't want to using Strong Will. A fact of life!

There will always be times at work when that happens as well as with your family and friends. It's knowing the appropriateness of doing what you don't want to do which counts.

Strong Will enables you to both do that which is right for you *and* the things you don't necessarily want to do but which are right to do in a bigger context.

Think of something at work recently which you didn't want to do but did.

Get a picture of yourself at that time and notice how you looked, sounded and felt.

Notice your facial expression and body posture, what your voice sounded like and what you said. And what were the feelings you had.... resignation, resentment, frustration, anger, hopelessness?

Notice how you carried out that task and how you behaved with other people because of how you felt?

HOLD that picture!

When you've developed Strong Will, carrying out that task you just thought about is a whole other ball game. And, one of the best ways to develop Strong Will is in your daily life.

For instance, if you were gardening, you would do it from outtayerbox YOU. You'd be present in the moment, being aware that each spadeful of earth you turn over is an act of Will. If you were washing up by hand, you'd be aware that each piece of crockery and cutlery you washed was an act of Will.

It's not just the acts of Will by Batman and Robin or real life people like Gandhi and Mandela which count... though reading their biographies is a real help in developing your own Strong Will. Acts of Will by everyday heroes and heroines count as well. Everyday heroes and heroines just like you!

Why do angels fly? Because they take themselves so lightly. And when you develop Strong Will through outtayerbox YOU, you can use it with playfulness, cheerfulness and curiosity.

Think again of that task at work which was so arduous for you.

Only, this time, imagine yourself approaching it from outtayerbox YOU using Strong Will as a potential learning experience.

In your mind's eye, you start thinking of every single act in the process of completing that task, every delegation and every management point as an act of Will.

And you approach the task with lightness and cheerfulness and the attitude of 'I wonder what I can learn about this or from doing this today?'

Again, notice how you look, sound and feel doing this task with Strong Will.

How different was that?

What have you learned from this comparison?

What will you do differently in the future?

The second aspect of overall Will is Skilful Will. It's not about what you do but how you do it. The idea is to achieve a task using the least amount of energy and effort possible.

If you think of systems and people at work, including yourself, you'll be able to identify cumbersome, uneconomical processes and people who make hard work of everything. They go about things the long way round and unnecessarily complicate them, perhaps, just to justify their existence.

In contrast, Skilful Will is an attitude you have to the task you're performing. Again, it comes from being outtayerbox YOU, present in the moment to yourself and things around you so you can assess how much energy you're putting into something.

Too little energy and it's like using a feather to lift a desk. Too much energy and it's like a construction site crane being used to raise up the same dumb bell.

The question always is, 'How can I most skilfully achieve what I want to from start to finish?' At work, as well as at home, for all kinds of projects that might include enlisting the help of other resources and other people... in a skilful way.

A project manager with whom I once worked was heavy handed with his team. There was no consultation with them or exploring and using their experience with similar projects.

He was also very territorial. So, there was no consulting either with people outside the team who would have had valuable input for the effectiveness of the project's outcome.

In addition, this manager micro-managed so the team felt undermined and deskilled by him. Needless to say, their energy and morale was rock bottom as people started, one by one, to look for other jobs.

In his work with me, he recognised his behaviour was totally unproductive and, indeed, harming. This was not an overnight success! It came out of several months' working together. And me challenging him to recognise his lack of self trust, his paranoia and a part of his personality he ended up calling The Control Freak.

He learned very tentatively to transform his heavy handed energy into the use of Strong, Skilful and Good Will... we'll come to Good Will next... to the bemusement of his team and delight of his management. There were, of course, other issues involved in the transformation but discovering, developing and using his Will in respectful relationship with himself and others was key.

And, your Will is not only for doing things.

For example, you might just choose to pass your time rather than do anything specific. And, even actively doing things is not strenuous or arduous when you make conscious, definite acts of Will in their doing. You'll discover instead that you feel energised, alive and more present in the world... outtayerbox YOU again!

Sometimes it's appropriate to act and sometimes it's appropriate not to act, to let things be. One of my favourite messages to my clients is that it's important to know when to mind your own business and when to let others mind theirs. You need to be flexible and find a balance between choices about doing and choices about not doing.

But, whether you do or do not, *whatever* you do or do not needs Good Will, the third and equally essential component of Will.

I can almost hear you spluttering *"Good Will!"* when you think of difficulties or people you find difficult at work. I had a wise old trainer once who, when I came across something I found unpalatable, would always say, "Trust me". It so rankled. Like she was going to show me, huh!

But, in fact, when I did learn to trust her, she did, indeed, show me the way. So, even though Good Will might sound not on or a bit woo-woo for you... trust me.

The more you practise being outtayerbox YOU, the more you will discover that being in the present, using your Will to make choices, somehow takes the sting out of situations. Where you might previously have got angry, had a tantrum, sulked or just generally felt pissed off with things, you're far calmer and you understand what's going on... even if you don't agree with it.

And you will have been using Good Will, even if you didn't know it at the time.

Without Good Will, Strong Will can be distorted into the bullying kind and Skilful Will into manipulation. Good Will underpins all your ethical and ecological use of Will.

An act of Good Will towards someone or something creates understanding and co-operation. It comes from awareness of yourself as not an isolated island but a member of a huge community of other people, creatures, organisations, systems and things.

It comes from your emotional and interpersonal intelligence as a member of the human race.

For just like that project manager, without Good Will you would take actions which only supported your own interests at the expense of others. And just like him, you could be suspicious of others, defensive and prejudiced against other people and other ways of doing things.

Alternatively, with too much Good Will towards others, things get distorted and you could get totally walked over.

You could so much want to act to help others that you could become a pain in the butt. People I work with who have this behaviour usually learned when growing up to be 'pleasers' or to be a 'good' girl or boy. All of them definitely have difficulty in saying 'no'.

End of!

You can develop Strong, Skilful and Good Will through behaving more and more from your outtayerbox YOU and achieving 100% high power ooomphing.

CHAPTER 20 – POWER
HIGH POWER OOOMPHING!

Our worst fear is not that we are inadequate, our deepest fear is that we are powerful beyond measure.

Marianne Williamson

Aligning your Will with your purpose and your passion creates high power ooomphing.

It results in you alive, present and visible in the world whether you do that in a big profile or low profile way. It results in you as a totally response-able and creative person who is at effect rather than at cause. It results in you standing in your own ground, choosing the contours and continents of your work, your life and way beyond.

It results in you making choices about how you are and what you do.

High power ooomphing doesn't have to show off. In fact, that's bravado, not power. Power is confident, self-assuring and, of itself, empowering for you and others.

> Take a moment to imagine yourself, see yourself as a high power ooompher at work. And notice how you look, how you sound, how you feel AND how other people respond to you.

So, what was your reaction to that exercise and the idea of you doing 'high power ooomphing'? Did you shrink back with horror? Did you make a vigorous air punch with one mighty 'Yay'? Or, are you totally indifferent wondering what the fuss is all about?

All of these reactions and yours, if it was different, are excellent clues as to what needs to happen for you to be totally at ease with using your Will and high power ooomphing. For you to be totally at ease with exactly how powerful you could be. Time to check it out...

> You'll be using your imagination again. So, get physically comfortable with your spine straight and feet square on the ground. Take a few deep breaths to relax. Close your eyes or look at the carpet or a blank wall to avoid any distractions.
>
> Be prepared to get pictures or a sense of 'something', even if it's not a concrete picture. Also be prepared to imagine through physical sensations or even sounds. Just trust your whole brain processing. It will send you exactly the information you need in the best form for you.
>
> Take another few deep breaths and then imagine that your Will is symbolised by a sword. And let the very sword which symbolises your Will appear right now in your imagination. Take whatever you get, however bizarre, without censoring.
>
> And if you get nothing, that's OK. A very astute American trainer once told me that blank, i.e., 'nothing', is very 'high space'. People meditate

their butts off to get there! Just stay with the 'nothing' and notice what emerges from it.

Now explore all the features of your sword.

From what is it made? Could be metal and could be something else.
What kind of handle does it have and what's it made from?
What's your sword's blade like, how big or small is it and what are its distinctive features?
If you drew your sword through the air, what sound would it make?
What condition is it in?
And how precisely does your sword feel in your hand?

Write down everything you can about what your sword is like.

Then go back to it and ask your sword the following questions...

What do you need me to know?

Jot down the answer, however bizarre, together with whatever words, pictures, sensations, feelings or sounds you get. Then ask your sword...

1. What aspect of your Will needs developing? Strong? Skilful? Good?

Could be all three, a combination of two or just one aspect.

2. What resources do you need to develop that aspect or aspects of Will?

3. And when you've developed that aspect, or those aspects, of Will, what gift will you have for me then?

Finish your conversation with your sword in anyway which feels right for you. When you have, allow your sword's image to fade knowing you can re-connect and imagine your sword any time you like.

What have you learned?

And what will you do differently in the future because of that learning?

If you're delighted by your sword and what you've discovered... good going. AND it's not unusual, when people first do this exercise, to feel disappointed in how their sword, their Will, appeared to them. If this is you... kick that gremlin out of the way right now.

Way back in the time of mystery out in Arabia lived a young boy. He was determined to create a life of fame and fortune for himself but was laughed at by his family and so-called friends.

They laughed at him as they didn't take his aspirations seriously because he was rather small for his size and puny in his physicality. And he knew he was a disappointment to his parents who longed for a vigorous and robust looking son.

The pain of this undermining eventually got to him one day. He found himself following a dusty trail out into the desert to get away from his town and the negative energy of those he knew. He walked and walked, kicking the sand beneath his feet first with frustration, then with anger and finally with tears of hurt for their disbelief in him.

And, while he was crying and kicking the sand, his foot hit against something sharp. So much so that it stung like hell and his tears were interrupted by howls of a stubbed toe as he hopped holding his foot in agony.

Finally, the pain and noise subsided. Curiously he limped to the point in the sand where he thought he'd come across the sharp object. And there he found a tip of dull metal poking out of the sand. Now on all fours, using his hands as shovels, he dug the metal object out.

Imagine his delight when he found a very dull, dented and mundane looking lamp. He'd heard the stories and, although he'd dismissed them as hocus pocus, with this old lamp in his hands

the superstitious side of him was very willing
to believe this was a magic lamp.

Using the corner of his head scarf he started
to give the lamp a rub, spitting on the metal in
the hope that would create a shine. He rubbed
and he rubbed but not a thing happened.
No magical sound. No magical shining. No
magical genie.

At first he was very disappointed. He berated
the lamp. "How could I ever think such a puny
old dented thing like you would hold a genie?
You're no good to me or anyone else!"

But because he'd already started developing
his outtayerbox YOU, it wasn't long before he
recognised what he was doing. And he began
to laugh and laugh at his own ludicrousness.
For he saw he was doing exactly to the lamp
what other people were doing to him through
disrespect and put-downs.

So, he changed his mood and attitude. Firmly
grasping the lamp he returned to his town
full of resolve to achieve his ambitions. With
courage and fortitude, he vowed to ignore
the undermining of those who could not see
beyond his physical self.

The lamp never did reveal a genie... if there
ever was one inside. But a very strange thing
happened instead.

As the boy kept developing his outtayerbox YOU, his purpose, passion and Will power, the dents in the old lamp were mysteriously hammered out. And as he grew into a man and began creating his journey to fame and fortune, the old lamp mysteriously became shinier and shinier.

Now, his idea of fame and fortune might not be yours or mine. For him it was to be renowned in the town for his learning, generosity and way with words. And it came to pass that his words spread and wealthy people hired him as a consultant and... Well, I think you'll know the rest.

When he fulfilled his ambition the old lamp shone so brightly it could have been made of diamonds. And he always kept his powerful lamp by his side to remember how things could change magnificently with self-development, purpose, passion and power.

So, honour your sword, however bright or dull it is, however splendid or shabby. It symbolises your Will and has gifts to bestow on you as you grow... which of course you will, won't you?

Again... take a moment to imagine yourself as a high power ooompher at work. Notice how you look, how you sound, how you feel and how others respond positively to you.

And notice how different your experiences are in this exercise compared to the one you did at the beginning of this chapter.

Make a note of those very positive differences.

Yes! I know it takes courage to do high power ooomphing at work, especially when it's new to you and other people.

And did you not have the natural courage to be birthed down a very narrow and constrictive canal? Did you not have the courage to stand to take those first wobbly steps which landed you on your butt? AND did you not have the courage to get up, again and again, and keep getting up until you mastered the skill of walking on two legs?

Did you not have the courage and Will to continue and triumph through practise practise practise?

You could say that was genetics and you had no choice with your birthing and physical development. You could say you just had to follow an organic and physical development programme.

Got it in one!

What makes you think, in the same way, that you're not genetically programmed to be true to yourself and live out your purpose, passion, power? Do you not keep getting called to be outtayerbox YOU through whacks around the head?

You can keep ignoring the calling for the rest of your life and pay the price only you can inevitably pay for denying yourself. The price you pay for not exerting the choice to be true to yourself and co-operating with your genetic programming to be outtayerbox YOU.

Your denial doesn't disprove that, in truth, there is really no choice *but* to fully live your purpose, passion and power.

For, you wouldn't be reading this book if that little voice, that urge, that push towards outtayerbox YOU and high power ooomphing wasn't something which bugs you from time to time.

More exploring...

> Draw a line down the middle of an A4 sheet of paper.
>
> Head up the left hand side with the question 'How do I stop myself from high power ooomphing at work?'
>
> And on each subsequent line write one way you do that.
>
> Examples could be... 'I get so caught up in office politics, I lose the point of what I'm trying to achieve', 'I get over-heated in discussions' and 'I tend to want to please authority figures all the time'.
>
> Keep writing even if you don't want to continue.

That's the very place to stay with it. Write rubbish if that's what comes. And, stick with it as that's the point you're probably reaching something juicy which the gremlins, trances or shticks don't want you to know.

When you've done, go back and look for similarities between some of your answers. Often they'll be connections between 'giving your power away' behaviours. Mark those which belong to each other when you find them.

Then ring the three 'giving your power away' behaviours which draw you to them the most.

And then mark one from the three which draws your attention to it the most.

Write that one on the left hand side of another sheet of paper. Draw a line down the middle and on the right hand side write the heading...

'How I can do it differently through high power ooomphing?'

Examples could be, 'I create reminders on my 'phone of what I'm trying to achieve politically', 'I manage my emotional state in discussions at all times through learning breathing practices' and 'I decide whether pleasing someone is right for me through understanding what lies behind my tendency with authority figures and managing my emotional state.'

What resources do you need to develop high power ooomphing in this area?

Resources could be external, like learning calming breathing practices, or eliciting a meeting with someone, or internal, like developing your courage or having your 'assertive' sub-identity around more of the time.

Set a date when you're going to take this first step in high power ooomphing. Tell someone trustworthy the date and what you're going to do. It always helps to enlist the support of someone to hold you accountable, particularly when you're going for a step change in behaviour.

Then, using your imagination, 'see' yourself on that date doing exactly what you plan to do.

Notice how you look, sound and feel and how other people respond positively to you. Rerun your imagining 'movie' at least three times ... and as many times as you want before doing it for real.

The mental rehearsal will have you totally primed and ready to successfully achieve your chosen act of high power ooomphing.

Celebrate when you've achieved it! It's so important to treat yourself in some delicious way to mark your triumph... any and all of your triumphs!

Recently I worked with a bright, young woman, relatively new to a post, who was supposedly being mentored by an older woman in her team. However, in discussing her job with the older women, she was dismayed to find that her 'mentor' took one of her ideas and presented it as her own at a meeting.

My client had chosen good naturedly to assume somehow it was an error on the older woman's part. However, when she did it again my client knew this was no error.

Feeling unable to confront the older woman, and with all trust in their relationship gone, my client had unsurprisingly been evasive and unwilling to open up in recent mentoring sessions. The older woman had felt it important to let their overall manager know the mentoring wasn't going as well as it could be due to my client's 'negative attitude'.

Resisting the urge to punch her in the face, my client chose to work with me to develop the skills to report matters to the overall boss and call the older woman on her behaviour. And our work followed much the same path as you're treading now to reach the point of high power ooomphing.

My client had previously felt disempowered, bursting with anger at the injustice of it all, and betrayed by the older woman who was supposed to be mentoring her. She hadn't yet developed the ability to stand powerfully in her ground to confront the situation and the 'players' in it.

Understandable, as, apart from office dynamics, confrontation itself is often thought to be a negative and potentially frightening experience. In fact, confrontation can be a very positive and healthy experience, as it certainly was in the end for my client. And it could have been for the older woman, if she'd been open to feedback.

Using her political intelligence, my client first approached her overall boss explaining, without blaming, what had led to her seemingly 'negative' attitude. She also told him she wanted to deal with the situation herself.

He agreed, partly because he was overloaded and grateful for one less thing with which to deal. Plus, it wasn't the first time he'd heard about this aspect of the older woman's behaviour. And, although my client wondered why he'd not previously called the older woman on it, she was wise enough not to raise that potentially sensitive issue.

Choosing an appropriate time and privacy, my client confronted the older woman, concluded their mentoring relationship and told her firmly never to steal another of her ideas again. The older woman ran to their overall boss with a story about my client's disrespectful behaviour.

However, of course, he was already aware of the situation and gave her short shrift. She never troubled my client again.

That's high power ooomphing ... which includes three special ingredients from ancient Greece.

CHAPTER 21 – ARISTOTLE HAD A THING OR TWO TO SAY...

'In the information age, you don't teach philosophy......
You perform it. If Aristotle were alive today he'd have a
talk show.'
Timothy Leary

I start writing this chapter wildly aware of how passionate I am for you to live from the freedom of outtayerbox YOU, to live from the freedom of your purpose, passion and power.

Imagine being passed in the street by a boy racer in his car. Although the windows are closed, you can hear his music, particularly the loud, deep, base boom boom boom. You can almost physically feel your eardrums vibrate with the unrestrained beat booming booming booming.

That's how passionate I am for your freedom from the penury of being inyerbox you, from living dead, from living a life unlived.

And, somehow, my passion is flooding out in this chapter like a torrent of water careering through canyons. A torrent that's intent on hijacking your canoe and shoving you through foam, waves, energy and places you've avoided until you land gasping and safe on the lush bank awaiting you downstream.

I'm fierce for you to live out your purpose passionately and powerfully at work.

I'm fierce for you to become an influential force not just for yourself but for all those with whom you come into contact.

For you to be able to inspire and motivate others to get outta*their*boxes and live *their* purpose with passion and power at work. And for those others to become influential forces, not just for their self but for all of those with whom they come into contact. To be able to inspire and motivate others to... Repeat, ad infinitum!

Get it?

It's the tumbleweed effect. The more it rolls, the more the tumbleweed grows in size by what it picks up along the way. And the bigger the tumbleweed grows...

... the more people who get whacked around the head and learn how to live life aloud, inter-dependently and collaboratively with each other and all life in our world...

That's how essential and valuable you are! Because it all starts with tumbleweed 'me'... in this case, tumbleweed YOU!

And, in order to create and promote this far more natural way of being and living, however hugely you do that or however small, you need to be able to influence both yourself and others.

You're already influencing yourself by learning to live from your purpose and to connect with and express your passion and power in healthy ways. And by your very being, what you say and do and how you say and do it, you can be a positive influencing energy for others too.

YES! I'll say it again... That's how essential and valuable you are for yourself and others.

And the last word in how to be ethically influential lies with Aristotle, a Greek philosopher who lived 384-322 BCE. Only he wasn't just a philosopher. He made enormous and important contributions to the fields of metaphysics, poetry, theatre, music, logic, rhetoric, politics, government, ethics, biology and zoology.

That's what I call influential!

Aristotle compiled his thoughts on rhetoric, the art of public speaking, including his theory of three persuasive 'appeals'. By that he meant the three essential ingredients you need to be an influential force, however big or small your sphere. Whether you want to be an influential force in global political arenas, in your work, in local communal affairs or within your own family.

His three essential ingredients are Ethos, Pathos and Logos.

Ethos is about your credibility as a person, creating an ethical appeal, convincing others by virtue of your character.

Pathos is about influencing through an appeal to your listener's emotions, getting them on board through experientially feeling what you're talking about.

Logos means influencing through reasoning, through the use of logical argument.

If we start with Ethos, think about a CEO, manager or boss for whom you've had little respect. They can talk a good talk but actually have little substance or real authority. Their ethics and values might be questionable.

And even though they might get things done their behaviour, in *how* they get things done *and* towards others, is less than desirable. You might even have come against the sharp edge of them yourself.

The question is... Were you influenced by this person or did you do what you had to do in the job despite them?

Because the heart of Ethos is about character. It's about your trustworthiness and credibility. It's about your reputation both as a human being, your record on integrity for example, and the work that you do, your expertise in your field.

Aristotle also points out the importance of good sense, good moral character and goodwill. By that, he does mean the kind of Good Will you read about in a previous chapter.

And, as you develop outtayerbox YOU, there's no way you won't be developing your character in line with what's highest and most commendable in you. There's no way you will want to act malevolently and out of self interest at the expense of others. There's no way you will want to coerce, play cheap political tricks or trample over people.

If you've behaved like that previously, well you've got a bit of reputation building and rebranding to do. At first, your co-workers or your staff will be suspicious, imagining your behaviour to be part of a new 'game plan'. Be consistent and eventually they'll accept you've changed for the better, delightfully so as far as they'll be concerned.

Pathos is about appealing to your audience's sympathy and imagination. It causes them not just to respond emotionally but to identify with your point of view, to feel what you feel. It refers both to the emotional and imaginative impact of your message on your audience.

I remember going to a business conference where there were some big name speakers. I was excited because I was seeing some of them for the first time. And, you know how it is, you have to choose which speakers' sessions to attend. So, I made my choices and turned up at my first speaker's slot.

He was certainly an expert in his field and had a good reputation for being a man who practised what he preached. He'd written several books to acclaim and was a by-word in his field. He was as dry as a bone!

He reminded me of the worst lecturers at university who just stood there and talked at you from notes. You might as well have read the notes yourself for all the impact the lecturer's presentation had on you. And, in this guy's case, I might just have well bought the book. Only I didn't because he was so damn boring.

I was luckier with the next speaker I'd chosen. She also had a great reputation in her field, turned up looking like a professional expert and had several books to her name. After that, there was no comparison. From the off she had me engaged, interested and up for what she had to say.

She created rapport with her audience, was warm, human and sometimes funny. She used anecdotes, stories, analogies, similes and metaphors to illustrate her points.

Her choice of words recreated the scenes which triggered my emotions in line with what she was talking about. She was also very engaged with her material which clearly demonstrated her values, beliefs and understanding of her topic.

Throughout she delivered herself and her material in an emotionally intelligent way so as to connect with her audience. And, by so doing, I was receptive to her ideas.

So in case you've been caught up in the buzz about emotional intelligence, it's nothing new. The Greeks and Aristotle were talking about it thousands of years ago!

Was I influenced by what she had to say? Yes. She made it easy for me to see and experience where she was coming from with her topic and to get her point of view. To this day I can remember some of what she said like, 'Never be afraid to be afraid. It just means you're learning!"

She clearly presented with Ethos and Pathos and an elegant smidgeon of Logos.

For logos is the logical appeal, to influence using cool reason, rational explanation and demonstrable evidence, either 'scientific' or experiential. Her message did, indeed, make sense and appealed to reason. Some of it used facts. Some of it used evidence from the field and the rest was gained through experiential exercises we did during her talk.

And, when she ended her presentation, I felt confident that the call to action she made for us to carry out could definitely lead to the outcome she promised. The rest was down to me taking that action!

If you're feeling a bit whacked about the head with the idea of developing Ethos, Pathos and Logos AND delivering it at work, I'm delighted. Time to move on...

CHAPTER 22 – HITLER HAD PURPOSE, PASSION AND POWER TOO...

'I believe firmly that in making ethical decisions, man has the prerogative of true freedom of choice.'

Corliss Lamont

Hitler also had a good dollop of Ethos. His credibility was amazingly high with his followers. And Pathos. My goodness how he could stir the emotions of the crowd. And Logos. Although his arguments seem fallacious to us, they weren't to the majority of German people at the time.

You only have to see him heading up a rally to understand how he had all the cards in the pack and was an impressive and influential orator. As have tyrants, despots and dictators been throughout time.

Imagine Hitler's purpose could have been something like, 'I bring heritage and purity for myself and others'. Imagine all the ways he could have turned his hypothetical purpose into action... compared with the way in which he actually did. Imagine all the ways in which he could have used his creative passion and essential power in line with that purpose... compared with how he actually did.

Reminds me of when I was doing the Genetics module of a psychology degree. The down to earth guy who was our lecturer, Ernie, if I remember rightly, greeted us something like this...

"Welcome to Genetics where you only have to understand one essential thing. If it can go right, it can also go wrong!"

In the same way, I'm unable to make you use the information in this book for your and the higher good. What you do with it will very much depend on your ethics, values *and* the level of your consciousness for yourself and others.

As I write that I'm reminded of a highly successful, big name 'trainer' in the world of Neuro-Linguistic Programming. And, if you haven't come across it, NLP is a body of philosophy, a zeitgeist and a vast pool of techniques which can be used for personal and professional development.

I experienced this trainer at an 'NLP' conference some years ago. My antennae started vibrating when I entered the session room before time to find him holding court with some fans. But, hey, the guy is a success and there's nothing like success to draw honey bees.

He began talking and, very quickly, I recognised he was using hypnotic language patterns designed to put you into trance *and* suggestibility. Very useful in a manipulative way for making sales!

Although feeling a little spaced out, early on, the woman sitting next to me and I had shared our recognition of what he was doing. So, we kept each other with both feet firmly on the ground most of the time with mutually administered physical nudges and digs.

I couldn't believe what I was hearing from this guy about using NLP to get your own way at other peoples' expense. This was a million miles away from the central tenets of NLP which advocate a philosophy of understanding and inclusiveness. And the pièce de résistance?

He told a story of buying trainers at a discount outlet where, through using hypnotic language patterns, he got the sales assistant to give him an even more and outrageous discount. I wouldn't have liked to have been that assistant post trance having to justify to their boss the extra discount on *that* transaction.

The trainer's behaviour left a bad taste in my mouth. But I guess he'd respond to my experience by crying all the way down to the bank. So much for Ethos!

Every field will have its rogues because of the simple truth... if it can go right, it can go wrong. There's not a theory or a system on earth which can't be used either for good or anti-good.

I once worked with a management consultant for whom the description snake-oil salesman would be conceived as generous. He presented himself as a very friendly, sincere and credible person. People naturally gravitated toward him because of his affability.

Yet, he could sell water as designer after-shave and not bat an eyelid. He used Ethos, Pathos and Logos purely for commercial gain.

However, he came my way through getting up one morning and, for the first time, truly seeing himself and his behaviour in the mirror. His awareness having been triggered through some honest feedback from close family and a true friend about his self-centredness and untrustworthiness.

The feedback, and seeing himself, created an almighty whack around the head which catapulted him into wanting to change for the better. He feared ending up as a lonely old man, despite all his wealth, because of his egocentric and cavalier behaviour.

I saw him once professionally as he was due to return to where he lived and worked abroad, not wanting sessions via the internet or telephone. And, although we only had the one session, he was at the point in a psychological crisis where a crack appears through which you can begin to see outtayerbox YOU.

That did, indeed, happen for him. And, in our several hours together, he became aware of his purpose and planned a way forward by choosing how he wanted to behave in the future. A truly whack around the head session!

I heard from him twice over a month or so via email after our work together. The first time, he was clearly still in remorse for his prior behaviour yet reported functioning pretty OK despite his distress.

On the second and last time I heard from him, he told me how much he liked himself again and felt totally back to normal. He also told me how much money he would make from two big upcoming deals.

He'd totally missed the point!

It wasn't about liking himself again or about getting totally back to normal as normal was before. It was about growing, expanding, leading a fuller and richer life *including* making loads of money if that's what he wanted.

It was about developing and then serving as a role model, showing his fuller, richer outtayerbox YOU so that others might be inspired to discover their own and live that way too.

As I mentioned in earlier chapters, there is always an urge to hang onto what we know rather than move forward into the unknown. We'll look at this more in the next chapter.

In this guy's case, it seems as though he didn't have the resources, internally or externally, to manage that challenge. In fact, he returned to a situation and a culture which would more likely support his old way of being rather than encourage him to develop the new.

The good news is that YOU cannot *not* behave ethically if you connect with AND take action to live as outtayerbox YOU! It's maintaining the connection and making choices about how you want to behave with yourself, and others, which makes all the difference.

So stay alert and awake to yourself. Stay vigilant. Watch out for any gremlins, trances or shticks getting involved in how you're using your purpose, passion, power and influence.

And when you recognise any of them getting in your way, give yourself

a multi-coloured and almighty whack around your head!

That's the best antidote I know to grandiosity and operating from bits of your personality which are anything from plain old screwed up to abusive.

And, as I go to talk about your own Ethos in more detail, I want to distract myself by stuffing my face with food... a highly successful trance inducing behaviour. It might be you've also got the feeling you'd like to skip the next bit.

Always, always, when I and you get a call to operate from the highest possible in us, we want to run. What if I don't live up to my expectations of myself? What if I slip up and crash? What if, what if, what if?

Just think. Whatever the nature of your work, whatever your position, how would it be to operate with purpose, passion and power AND be influential in not only providing a model to inspire others but also to inspire yourself?

Because, then you'll truly be inspirational. And you'll discover living in the best way you can will also inspire and motivate you to keep on that path and develop it even more.

So, create a much huger desire for good alongside your desire for avoidance and the desire for good will win every time. As I write that, I don't want to stuff my face anymore and my guess is you'll also be re-engaged and raring to go. So....

> Think of a situation at work in which you could be influential.

> Consider all the factors in that situation until you've got all the information you need to provide the foundation for you to consider how you can be influential in resolving it.

> Now...

> Consider Ethos and all the plus factors you have to be a credible and respected person in that situation. Make a list.

> Consider your reasons for wanting to influence this situation. Is it purely for personal gain? Is it to get one over a colleague? Or is it motivated to improve things for yourself and others in line with the greater good?

> And are you acting in line with Strong, Skilful and Good Will?

> Consider Pathos. What are the anecdotes you could tell, and the emotional experiences you could create, to engage the feelings of people

involved directly in that situation? And how could you appeal to their feelings in line with resolving it?

Consider Logos. What rational case could you put forward for the resolution of this situation? Think about key reasons and logical arguments which support your case, including any factual evidence if you have it. Think about the language you'll use and how you'll present yourself as the speaker who's taking the lead on this situation.

Now...

Imagine yourself successfully and influentially speaking to other people about resolving the situation. Notice how you look, how you sound, how you feel AND how other people respond positively to you. Spend several minutes in this creative imagining.

When you've done, give yourself a big shake. Come out of your imagination and be fully awake in your present reality.

Repeat the previous imagining and when you've done so...

Again, give yourself a shake and come back. Then...

Imagine being a successful influencer once more, relishing your achievement as you influence the situation elegantly and easily.

Give yourself a last shake and come back again....

Notice how you're feeling right now ... and celebrate your success!

It might be, through the process of imagining, you noticed other resources you need or ways to tweak what you're saying or doing. In which case, adapt your imagining to include them. Then repeat the process.

And once you've got influencing the situation the best that you can imagine... GO DO IT!

I feel passion stirring in me for you being an influential and effective force at work and in the rest of your life.

The wonderful thing is that whatever you do you're going to do it 'right'. Because, even if you don't get it quite right, according to what you think is 'right', or you screw up completely, you'll learn loads from it which will help you develop being outtayerbox YOU even more. There's no righter way to be...

Who me?

YES... YOU!

In whatever big or small ways you chose to use your purpose, passion and power...

CHAPTER 23 – So, What If Change Is Scary! The fear

'Change is inevitable except from a vending machine.'
Robert C. Gallagher

So far so good. You've been reading and doing, or not doing, the exercises. You'll also have been receiving an occasional whack around the head, or not, depending on the level at which you're reading this book. And now?

And now, if you haven't done so already, is the time to START DOING SOMETHING ABOUT IT.

Wait. I'll just rewind myself... because you do have a choice.

You might be one of those people who read personal and professional development books as an intellectual exercise. You get the concepts and you can see what following the book's guidance will beneficially result in. But that's as far as it goes.

Why?

Because every time you stretch yourself you get scared. Every time you embark on something new and important to you, you get scared. Every time you set yourself a challenge which is just a bit more than you're used to, you get scared.

Being scared at the thought of getting out of your comfort zone gets adrenalin coursing through your body. Your heart beats faster. You could even feel a little nauseous from the quivering in your belly. And that's healthy. It's giving you a boost of nervous energy to apply to your stretch and achieve it.

Yet, more usually, you'll see your fear as an uncomfortable, if not nasty or hated, feeling to be got rid of rather than included and appreciated. Although, there are 'adrenalin junkies' who get their rocks off challenging themselves so frequently that being scared becomes a way of life.

Wasn't that way for me. I remember being told as a child not to walk on the top of a small wall because I'd fall off and hurt myself. So what! The worst I could do was scrape and bruise myself. And the very best I could do would be to learn from my tumble how to walk on top of small walls in a far more skilled way.

However, this and other warnings ended up with me fearful. I learned how to cling to what was familiar to me rather than risk the unknown and 'hurting' myself. Fearful and clinging? Frustrated, miserable and unfulfilled as well.

I've often heard from leaders and managers that, when they first took on a new role or got the step-up job, they were terrified. They expanded a lot of energy acting 'as if' they could do the job while not sure they could. They walked around with anxiety gnawing at their bones until time passed and they became more familiar with the role and themselves in it.

So, if you think about all the times you've felt scared and done the thing anyway, did anything terrible happen at work? My guess is probably not.

I've also heard people say that they're scared of change in case their family, friends and/or work colleagues won't like it and won't 'love' them anymore. While 'love' might sound a bit strong for the work context, it's the probable underlying motivation for wanting to be liked, to be one of the boys or to be one of the 'in crowd'.

Reality is that some of those people won't even notice you've changed. They're so intheirbox with their own perceptions of the world and agendas that they won't even register you've become a far more refined version of yourself.

And, if anyone doesn't like the changes in you, what are you going to do? Change back? I don't think so.

Once you've discovered the benefits of living from your outtayerbox YOU, your purpose, passion and power, the chances are you will never ever want to go back to your old and hobbled way of being. Remember... chickens can fly!

And what might happen if you don't embrace change? There's one very simple answer. Staying where you are risks death of some kind.

Think of people you've known at work who haven't challenged and expanded themselves. They're people who've done the same, or similar, jobs day after day, in the same old same old way. who've become resistant to change.

When supermarkets were in their infancy, the writing was most definitely on the wall for the small independent grocer. Some were savvy enough to get 'taken over' and secure their future. Some were savvy enough to sell up to someone far less savvy than they were.

And some lost their shirts, or went bankrupt, through not recognising the grocery trade in the UK was rapidly evolving in line with the USA. I know because my grandfather and uncle, joint owners in a grocery business, were amongst those who were so resistant to change they denied it.

And, as I write, British Airways cabin crew intend to strike protesting about changes needed to cut costs so the company survives. At the very time when the company needs to keep faith with the flying public and survive financially, strikes prevent flights which could sound the death knell for the company.

The old saying holds water. Next to death and taxes, the only constant in life is that it changes. And if you aren't willing to cope with the scariness of change, you're going to be left behind. Because, one way or another, change is inevitable.

Your company merges with another and jobs are on the line. The market place your company serves changes due to technological advances. You get a promotion. You get made redundant. Circumstances demand you get with the programme or ship out.

Think of a time you resisted change because you were scared.

What was that about?

What did you fear?

And what was the 'death', real or metaphorical, which came about from you resisting change?

If you look back over your life, how familiar is that fear? And how familiar is that outcome?

I think it was Einstein who said to keep on doing the same old things and expect to get different results is the definition of insanity. So, if that's been you, what do you need to manage the feeling of being scared AND 'go for it' at the same time?

Most often, clients give me one or two answers to that question. Usually, the first answer is that they need courage. And, if there's a second answer, it's normally the need for reassurance that, if they go for change and step out in to the unknown, it's all going to be OK.

And the wonderfully crazy thing is, if you embrace change, all will be well... however things turn out.

CHAPTER 24 – So, What If Change Is Scary! Ride like Sir Lancelot

'The interval between the decay of the old and the formation and the establishment of the new, constitutes a period of transition which must always necessarily be one of uncertainty, confusion, error, and wild and fierce fanaticism.'

John C. Calhoun

In mythic history, Sir Lancelot du Lac is considered to be one of the greatest and most trusted of King Arthur's knights who contributed to many of the king's victories. He's probably most famous for his role in searching for the Holy Grail... and for being intimate with the king's wife.

In all matters, Sir Lancelot is generally regarded as one of the most courageous knights at the Round Table. As for the Holy Grail, if only he'd known it was totally in his reach within himself rather than seeking it in the outer world. It's also not a million miles from re-discovering and living from outtayerbox YOU.

Whatever Lancelot's areas for improvement, he certainly was a man's man, sometimes depicted astride his horse and riding boldly whatever his challenge. For when it comes to change being scary...

Being FIERCE is the absolute opposite of being FEAR-FULL!

Years ago, I had a trainer who'd gone to New York on business. She and her colleague were returning from a networking dinner on foot and took a short cut. This was a big mistake because their knowledge of New York's geography was not the best. And, sure enough, before too long they found themselves lost.

More than that, they were well off the main blocks and both became anxious to find their way back to civilisation. Where they were walking, now very quickly, was quiet and eerie and both became fearful.

My trainer thought she'd found the way back and hurried them both down a dark alley which did, indeed, have sight of busyness and main route traffic at the very end of it. However, they only got mid-way when a guy jumped out of the shadows, with what looked like a gun pointing at them, and demanded money.

Afterwards, my trainer couldn't explain rationally why she'd done what she did. But, in that moment of danger, she opened her mouth and gave out the loudest and most ferocious roar her colleague said he'd ever heard. Not only that, but her body took the shape of a foraging ogre as if about to pounce and eat its prey.

The mugger froze in shock, a horrified look on his face. And, as my trainer was winding herself up for another almighty roar, he turned on his heels and ran away from them like someone possessed.

I guess what determined this outcome was my trainer behaving totally but totally unexpectedly. What can't be explained is how she 'got' that being fierce is not only a great antidote to being fear-full, it's also a great deterrent.

Perhaps, in the back of her mind, she remembered the New Zealand rugby team. For they perform the now famous Maori Haka at the beginning of matches to put the fear of god into their opponents. Now that's *really* fierce!

It involves roaring in unison, stamping feet in unison, the rolling of huge eyes and the concerted poking in and out of tongues ferociously. And it's a sure fire way to wind yourself up into fierceness.

I'm delighted to let you know you can also cultivate courage through tapping into being fierce. Ok! So, I looked it up and discovered fierce is defined as...

menacingly wild, savage, or hostile... violent in force, intensity like in 'fierce winds'... furiously eager or intense as in fierce competition. I love it so much here are some words having the same or nearly the same meaning...

> Untamed; cruel, fell, brutal; barbarous,
> bloodthirsty, murderous, violence of temper,
> manner, or action: fierce in repelling a foe.
> Ferocious implies fierceness or cruelty, esp. of
> a bloodthirsty kind, in disposition or action: a
> ferocious glare. Furious, passionate, turbulent.

As we've seen before with passion and Will, 'fierce' is a word which gets a very bad press. When, in fact, 'fierce' is just an energy which can be used for good, as with my trainer, or not good, as with, for example, extreme extremists on the political right or left of any culture.

And the superb give-away right at the bottom of that list is 'passionate'. For when you connect with your fierceness, you connect with your passion and then courage is only a sliver away.

> Think of a situation at work where you're fearful about someone or something.

> Write down or draw all the factors which make it scary for you... including any gremlins, trances or shticks.

> Now just put your list to one side and give your body a good wriggle like a dog shaking off water to get rid of your list's energy.

> Trusting outtayerbox YOU, take three deep breaths to relax. Go into your imagination, eyes closed or open. And now let outtayerbox YOU give you an animal, bird or human, real or fictional, alive or dead, which symbolises your FIERCENESS for you.

> Take whatever you get, however bizarre, without making it more 'polite' or 'sensible'. Please, please let your symbol be!

> My symbol for fierceness is a bloodied and victorious Atilla the Hun. So if you get one as raw

and pictorial as that, or even more, keep it. And if you don't, that's OK too.

If your symbol shows up pink and fluffy then gremlins, trances or shticks have definitely sabotaged your exploration. So thank them politely and tell them that, right now, you're going to imagine your fierceness in all its glory. And go again.

Explore your symbol for fierceness... its shape, its colours, how it looks, how it sounds, how it moves, how it operates out in the world. Explore anything but anything you can observe about your fierceness.

When you've finished doing that, step into your fierceness in your imagination and, in real time now, let your body immediately move into the position it wants to for being fierce. Move around noticing how powerful and energising it is to be fierce you.

You might even want to ham it up, with some roaring or gestures, which will give you an even more delicious taste of how your fierceness is and feels.

When you've had enough, step out of fierce you. Then write or draw some notes and key words as a record. You can use it to remind yourself any time in the future what your fierceness is like and how to reconnect with it when you want to.

Lastly, bearing in mind Strong, Skilful and Good
Will, together with Ethos, Pathos and Logos,
imagine being fierce you in the situation with
which you began this exercise.

See yourself in your mind's eye operating out of
Outtayerbox YOU and being fierce you for the
good of yourself and others in that situation.

Notice how you look, how you sound and
how you feel. And how other people respond
positively to you.

Now return from your imagining and write or
draw what you observed and what happened
when you used your fierceness in that situation.

Then...

With great delight, tear up the list you wrote of
all the factors which had made that situation
scary. Tear it up into tiny, tiny shreds and destroy!
Those factors are no longer relevant or true.

Lastly...

What did you learn?

And what will you do differently in the future
because of your learning?

Congratulations once more. Connecting with FIERCE you helps you connect with courageous you. And the secret is being fierce and being courageous doesn't mean you're not afraid.

In fact, as in the exercise you've just done, being aware of and feeling your fear is the starting point to connect with your fierceness and courage. The difference is you take *charge* of your fear rather than having it take charge of you.

CHAPTER 25 – So, What If Change Is Scary! Who knows?

'A fear of the unknown keeps a lot of people from leaving bad situations.'

Kathie Lee Gifford

One of my son's favourite sayings is 'hindsight is a perfect science'. And that's true for all of us. Once you've lived through a change, making decisions within it, then and only then can you look back and check out whether it was a wise or less than wise move that you made.

Actually, I believe every move you make, every decision you make, every change and situation you navigate is a wise move. Whatever you did, you did the best you could, at that time, with the internal and external resources you had then. And, whatever you did or did not would have taken you on a learning journey.

So, your desire from the last chapter to know all will be well after change just comes from the fear of moving out of your comfort zone. It comes from moving from the familiar into the vast unknown.

> An incredibly long time ago in ancient China there was a farmer who ran his small-holding with the help of his only son and one horse. And though times could be hard, the farmer

was successful making enough money to keep
himself and his son well.

Regrettably, this was not so for his neighbours
who didn't work with strength, skill or
goodwill. And who spent rather too much
of their time in idle gossip only too eager to
maliciously gloat or envy their more ethical
and hardworking peers.

One night a ferocious storm hit the hamlet
and the farmer's horse, rearing in fright, broke
free from his tethering, galloped up into the
hills and away. Well, the very next morning the
neighbours noticed its absence and enquired
what had happened.

They realised that, without a horse, the farmer
would have severe difficulties in working his
smallholding. And insincerely, like a wailing
choir, they exclaimed, "*HOW* unfortunate!"

However, the farmer, knowing the ways of
things, just shrugged his shoulders and replied,
"Who knows?"

The very next day the farmer's horse galloped
snorting and fiery back into his home yard
and brought with him a mate he'd attracted
while away in the hills. And this time the
neighbours rushed round, coo-ing and baying
obsequiously, "Oh how very fortunate! Now
you have two horses to work your land."

And the farmer, taking it all in his strides, shrugged his shoulders and replied, "Who knows?"

The farmer left the job of taming the wild horse to his only son who began it with relish. However, he made the mistake of not listening carefully enough to the wild horse or communicating with her in such a way that she understood what was needed.

And it wasn't long before she reacted by rearing violently again and again. The farmer's son on her back did his best to hold onto the bucking bronco. Alas, not well enough. With a final, wild arching and rearing, the wild horse threw him to the ground where he broke his leg.

You can imagine the neighbours' reaction. Always with an eye out for what was happening on the farmer's land, they ran right over with syrupy protestations of sorrow. "Oh no! You're declining in years and without your young, strong son you'll be unable to work your land. *HOW* unfortunate!"

The farmer eyed them with a seasoned look and shrugged his shoulders as he gave his habitual response, "Who knows?"

It wasn't long before the Chinese army came riding through the province.

They visited every town, every village and every hamlet forcefully conscripting all the young men into the army for a coming campaign of war. The only young man in the whole province to have escaped the conscription was the farmer's son due to his broken leg.

If the truth be told, those neighbours were beside themselves having had their sons taken away. However, it didn't stop them from rushing over to the farmer's small holding and crowing about his luck... "How very, very, very fortunate," they exclaimed.

And the farmer, with one wry look at his neighbours and a tender look at his son, shrugged his shoulders and replied.... "Who knows?"

Indeed! A fortuitous thing can turn out not so good as well as excellently. And a not-fortuitous thing can turn out excellently as well as not so good. Who knows?

What I do know is developing your outtayerbox YOU, your own inner leadership, and your purpose, passion and power is a fortuitous thing which cannot *not* turn out no good!

So you might be scared... good! Remember, it means you're coming out of your comfort zone. Just as I did way back in my early thirties. And that means nothing will ever, ever be the same again... even if it is.

Let's use the Chinese farmer's story for a moment. Inyerbox you reads it as just a story which, of course, it is on the surface. Outtayerbox YOU understands so much more from it than just the story.

Where's Purpose in the Chinese farmer's tale?

And where can you recognise Passion at work in the story?

And who's got the Power here... the ability to observe in an impartial way, make ethical and ecological decisions and take action with Strong, Skilful and Good Will?

And now...

What do you recognise from the story which relates to you at work, the work itself, your workplace, your colleagues and the organisational dynamics and politics?

Overall, what's your major learning from this exercise?

And how have you and your perceptions changed through doing this exercise?

What will you do differently in the future at work because of your learning and your perceptual changes?

So, you see, change can be a growth-full and positive experience. It depends what you do with it. And, as change is a more likely fact of life in 21st Century work, you better get used to it.

Once upon a time you could, if you chose, work for one employer all your life. A job in a bank was much prized as it also came with a safe pension at the end of it. Most people, even if they did move around, did one kind of job for the whole of their working life.

There was a sense of constancy and safety... even if it was an illusion. Which it was. In reality we can never know for sure what's going to happen from minute to minute, let alone in the future.

So, the illusion is definitely shattered now. If you're not able to adapt and grow, you'll fall by the wayside. The way forward is to be in life-long learning, developing personally and professionally, and able to have serial careers if need be.

I had a case in point this week. My washing machine ground very noisily to a devastating halt and I called in the same washing machine repair man I've used for something like 25 years. He arrived cheery and positive as always.

However, things had changed. The company he'd worked for had gone bust so he'd had to do more work privately. And that wasn't constant enough for financial security.

Being the ethical man he is, he told the truth about needed repairs and didn't exaggerate on his fees either.

So, no way he was going to rip off his clients for more money.

He knew he wasn't an entrepreneur. He didn't want to develop the work through strategic alliances or building a company. What he wanted was to do his job, earn enough money to take care of his expanding family and come home at the end of the day with his wages earned. So, what to do?

Simple! He looked at his skills, including those he could develop, and explored what jobs were on the market. Then he married the two.

So, he now had his private washing machine repair work, including odd bits of work for companies when they needed extra staff, and he drove local borough council vehicles which he loved.

In fact, his second job was even more in line with his purpose, passion and power. As a caring man, he did the pre and after school run for children with special needs and found this the most fulfilling part of all his work.

Change happened and he'd embraced and adapted to it. The most intelligent and creative thing you can do. Because the beautiful crazy thing is, when you get fierce and embrace change, all is and will indeed be well... even if you don't consciously know it at the time.

And that's true for change within... as well as without!

While the scariness of change might mean you fear wetting yourself, or you do, indeed, wet yourself, it also offers you the superb opportunity to buy new and up to the minute designed under-garments. Substantial ones created through connecting with and developing your outtayerbox YOU, your purpose, your passion *and* your power.

So where ever you are in your growth through this book, it's time to explore the 'who knows?' of how the changes you've made have influenced or can influence the quality of your experience at work. And if you don't think you've changed at all, be prepared to be delighted and surprised by what you discover...

CHAPTER 26 – EVEN MORE SO!
PART I

... is a delicious linguistic device used in Turkey to build on a compliment or success for yourself and/or another. It's a wish for even more of that particularly 'good' thing to come your way.

And that's my wish for you from all the whacks around the head you've had up to now in your life and have yet to arrive. Future whacks which, hopefully, through reading this book, won't totally knock your door down and demolish your building.

I wish you even more so of those particularly good things which emerge from the whacks to come your way... and the non-whacks.

So, time for self assessment which is not the kind you're used to for those annual appraisals.

They're potentially an excellent opportunity to affirm yourself for what you've done great and explore areas of yourself at work where you could be even better. But they leave out whole swathes of information you could harvest with whole brain processing as you've been using with this book. And will use for your assessment right now.

Perhaps, in fact, we need to change the words 'self assessment' which smack of all the associations you put on that yearly appraisal which doesn't always live up to its potential. How about calling it a 'dynamic valuation-appreciation' instead?

Give yourself about sixty minutes or more, if you can, for the whole process. It's important you do it from start to finish in one go. This will help you keep contact with the flow of energy the dynamic valuation-appreciation will stimulate.

<u>Phase One</u>

The first step is to use logical, mental intelligence to answer the following questions.

If you're unsure of what a question is asking you, just go with whatever you think it means. What's important is the answer you give yourself. What's totally irrelevant and unimportant is trying to work out any intention I might have in asking the question. In fact, by now, I hope you're more than used to things not always being clear!

How well have I developed outtamybox ME and how could I do it even better?

How well have I developed my Purpose and how could I do that even better?

How well have I developed my Passion and how could I do that even better?

244

How well have I developed my Power and how could I do that even better?

And, for each of the above, are there any resources, internal or external, which could help you to develop even more so?

Notice how you feel as you finish answering the above questions.

Now put your answers away and out of sight.

<u>Phase Two</u>

With this book in your hands and, at your own pace, begin flicking through pages from the very beginning. Or, if you're using a reader, scroll through pages in a similar way.

Let your eyes catch whatever they want to catch. This could mean you'll linger longer on some pages or sections than others. This could also mean you'll re-read pieces here and there.

Just trust outtayerbox YOU and do whatever the urge is to do as you go through this book. And when you've done...

On a fresh piece of paper, answer all the questions in Phase One again but, this time, with whatever comes freely into your mind as an answer. Please let the words, imaginings, symbols, sensations and even sounds flow naturally. Record them as accurately as you can.

For example, when I thought about the Purpose question for myself I 'saw' a fore-arm and clenched hand swing into a massive air punch. What that means *for me* is by the very act of writing this book, these very words I write now, I'm celebrating and honouring my Purpose. This book is my purpose in action.

So, take whatever you get even if you don't understand it as you record it. In the moments, hours or days ahead you will.

When you've recorded all your answers, including what resources you might need, notice how you feel. Then record that too.

<u>Finally... Phase Three</u>

Compare your feelings now with the feelings you had when you answered these self same questions in Phase One.

What's different?

What have you learned?

And what will you do differently in the future because of your learning?

My guess is the second time around you felt 'even more so'. My guess is there was a different and deeper quality to your feelings and, perhaps, even a quiet sense of 'rightness' or being at peace with yourself and what you're about.

Perhaps even a deep connection which goes even beyond outtayerbox YOU and yourself.

Stay at this point. Relish your feeling experiences until you're truly ready to read on....

Chapter 27 - Even more so!
Part II

For 'even more so' includes even more of who you are, what you are and how you can be. 'Even more so' includes what you can positively contribute at work and elsewhere in your life for your own good and that of others.

So, what do I mean by 'contribution'?

In the first place, I know, if you've followed this book through, you will be experiencing purpose, passion and power at work right now. You will be a changed person from the one who first picked up this book. Whether that's a massive change or a small one is immaterial. You know a way forward from where you were to where you are now... and where you want to go.

It's certainly not the only way. But it's a way I've found immensely valuable and, if you worked your way through, I believe you will have discovered its value too.

If that's so, you now have knowledge of a way which might, at the right time and when appropriate, also help other people to move from 'living dead' or 'asleep' or 'in trance', or whatever, to being fully alive.

Contribution is offering your learning and your 'being' for the good of yourself and others. In this case it's a way of 'paying forward', being of service to yourself and others, now and in the future.

For example, if I decorate your lounge which, by the way, is highly unlikely, instead of asking for a fee I could ask you to take my 'good deed' forward. So you, in turn, would do a good deed for someone else in the future.

My good deed then results in a whole string of good deeds from you and the people *you* help. And then the people *they* help... and so on. Paying me forward abundantly!

And as you operate more and more from outtayerbox YOU, your purpose, passion and power, you cannot *not* begin to perceive your life and what you do as meaningful. Even if you're still in the job which you experienced as dispiriting not so long ago.

Whatever your current job, it's a vehicle through which you can turn into real life action your purpose, passion and power, even if you haven't yet worked out how. And, by so doing, you will experience your working life so much richer than it was when you began to read this book.

Find the work not challenging enough? What's your purpose and how can you use it to have the work be more challenging? And, how can you engage your purpose and passion to achieve that right now?

Not want to stay in your current job? Use it to learn how to live life fully right now while you're looking for your new job. It's a great practise ground for whatever you move onto next. If you can do it in this job, you can do it in any job.

Working with people who are difficult? Again, what's your purpose and how can you use it together with your passion and power to deal with people you've previously found difficult?

Feel that you've got so much more to give? Then line yourself up with your purpose, passion and power and explore what that 'much more' is and how you can 'give it' at work right now.

There's absolutely, but absolutely, no reason or excuse for not living 'even more so' now. And, if you find that incredible, go back to basics. Wheedle out those gremlins, trances and shticks which get in your way of doing the work and of living the life you both desire and deserve.

YES... YOU CAN!

And to prove it... be prepared to be surprised and delighted!

Sit with both feet on the ground and your back straight. Either close your eyes, or look at some blank space, to avoid distractions.

Take a few deep breaths, and gently relax your body, feelings and mind until you find the quietest and stillest spot inside from which to start imagining.

Now, on your imagination mind screen, see yourself at work a month or two down the line. You finished reading this book a month or two earlier and continue using what it taught you to develop yourself professionally and personally. You might even dip back into it from time to time.

Now, notice your work situation and what's going on around you.

'See' yourself operating from outtayerbox YOU, in line with your purpose, passion and power. Notice how you look, how you sound and how you feel.

Notice what you're saying and how you conduct yourself at work AND how others respond positively to you.

Now, take a mental snapshot of yourself in that the scene with all its ingredients.

Then come back into the room...

What did you notice about yourself in the future that you haven't noticed before?

What did you learn about yourself going into the future?

And what will you know to do differently because of that learning?

Congratulations!

If you can imagine yourself successfully being outtayerbox YOU not so far ahead, I guarantee you will and, perhaps, are even now without realising it.

You can, indeed, find your purpose, passion and power at work *right now*!

THE END

That's it...

You're done!

If that seems even just a little whack around the head, you probably wanted a roundup of... well, of whatever you wanted a roundup of. Maybe the content... a nice, tidy, ticked-boxes package with which to finish.

But, just like death, all you're being offered is a full stop.

Or are you?

For, just as when you passed your driving test, got your professional qualifications or took on a new role, it was the end of what went before and the beginning of what is to come.

The rest is now completely and absolutely up to you!

ABOUT THE AUTHOR

Sharon Eden wanted to be a writer and actress but bamboozled herself in her 20s, through a desire for 'normality' and 'respectability', into a corporate career in sales and marketing in the wine trade.

Several whacks around the head in her 30s, fuelled by curiosity about what made her and other people tick, led her to higher education, studying psychology. She later qualified as a psychotherapist, then coach and trainer.

Sharon's credentials include MA Psychotherapy, Member Institute of Directors, Founding Member Association for Coaching, Member European Mentoring and Coaching Council, UKCP Registered

Psychotherapist, Registered Trainer INLPTA, Member Applied Psychology Association and Charter Member International Positive Psychology Association.

She's been told that her skills and presence as a writer and actress, allied with absolute passion for her topic, are woven indelibly through her roles. They contribute to making her a dynamic, enlightening, humorous and sometimes surprising presenter, speaker and trainer.

Sharon lives in a suburb of London, UK, and is lucky enough to be 20 minutes' train ride into town and 5 minutes' drive from the country. Both of which, together with delicious family and friends, nourish her and her appetite for life.

Connect with her at www.sharoneden.biz and @sharoneden on Twitter.

Lightning Source UK Ltd.
Milton Keynes UK
07 January 2011
165325UK00001B/1/P